Cross-Stitch
the Special
Moments
in Your Life

Cross-Stitch the Special Moments in Your Life

Marie Barber

Sterling Publishing Co., Inc. New York
A Sterling/Chapelle Book

Chapelle Ltd.

Owner: Jo Packham

Editor: Leslie Ridenour

Staff: Marie Barber, Malissa Boatwright, Kass Burchett, Rebecca Christensen, Holly Fuller, Marilyn Goff, Amber Hansen, Michael Hannah, Shirley Heslop, Holly Hollingsworth, Susan Jorgensen, Pauline Locke, Barbara Milburn, Linda Orton, Karmen Quinney, Cindy Rooks, and Cindy Stoeckl

Photography: Kevin Dilley, photographer for Hazen Photography

Photo Stylist: Susan Laws

All frames were painted by Marie Barber. Scroll saw work on frames was done by Tom Hamm.

Acknowledgements: Projects in this book were made with products provided by the following manufacturers: DMC Floss, Gay Bowles Mill Hill Beads, Kreinik, The Artist Touch, Wichelt Fabrics, and Zweigart Fabrics.

Library of Congress Cataloging-in-Publication Data

Barber, Marie.
   Cross-stitch the special moments in your life / Marie Barber.
     p. cm.
   "A Sterling/Chapelle book."
   Includes index.
   ISBN 0-8069-9612-9
   1. Cross-stitch--Patterns. I. Title.
TT778.C768365 1997
746.44'3'041--dc21
                                            97-2479
                                           CIP

10 9 8 7 6 5 4 3 2 1

A Sterling/Chapelle Book

Published by Sterling Publishing Company, Inc.
387 Park Avenue South, New York, NY 10016
© 1997 by Chapelle Ltd.
Distributed in Canada by Sterling Publishing
C/o Canadian Manda Group, One Atlantic Avenue, Suite 105
Toronto, Ontario, Canada M6K 3E7
Distributed in Great Britain and Europe by Cassell PLC
Wellington House, 125 Strand, London WC2R 0BB, England
Distributed in Australia by Capricorn Link (Australia) Pty Ltd.
P.O. Box 6651, Baulkham Hills, Business Centre, NSW 2153, Australia
Manufactured in the United States of America
All Rights Reserved

Sterling ISBN 0-8069-9612-9

If you have any questions or comments or would like information about any specialty products featured in this book, please contact:

Chapelle Ltd., Inc.
P.O. Box 9252
Ogden, UT 84409

Phone: (801) 621-2777
FAX: (801) 621-2788

"The essential elements...of the romantic spirit are curiosity and the love of beauty."
—Walter Pater

Marie Barber lives in Ragland, Alabama, on the Coosa River with her husband of eight years and their year-old daughter. Marie was born and raised in Kristianstad, Sweden.

Art and needlework have been part of her life since she was just a young girl, both at home and at school where, from the third to the ninth grade, the children—girls and boys—were required to study needlework.

Marie says she has always loved to draw and illustrate. At the age of 14, she was the youngest student to study oil painting under the instruction of the late Dr. Göran Trönnberg.

She came to the United States for the first time in 1983 as an exchange student. In 1987, Marie was accepted to the Art Institute of Atlanta. She has freelanced as a novel illustrator for a Swedish weekly publication and some of her artwork is featured in Loretta Goodwin's Gallery at Birmingham, Alabama. Although she has explored several avenues of the art world, Marie says she found her passion in 1993 when she began designing cross-stitch patterns and soon after ventured into needlepoint, hardanger, and silk ribbon embroidery.

Contents

The good things in life are not to be had singly, but come to us with a mixture.

Introduction

The pieces in this book are divided into four sections. Each section begins with photographs of the pieces in that section. The first page of each piece includes a reference to the page number where the accompanying photograph can be found.

Please pay special attention to information provided with each graph. There are some cases in which one or more graphs share the same code and/or photograph.

Several pieces include optional designs for stitching and additional verses that may be stitched to accompany the larger piece.

Fabric for Cross Stitch

Counted cross stitch is usually worked on even-weave fabrics. These fabrics are manufactured specifically for counted-thread embroidery and are woven with the same number of vertical as horizontal threads per inch.

Because the number of threads in the fabric is equal in each direction, each stitch will be the same size. The number of threads per inch in even-weave fabrics determines the size of a finished design.

Number of Strands

The number of strands used per stitch varies depending on the fabric used. Generally, the rule to follow for cross-stitching is three strands on Aida 11, two strands on Aida 14, one or two strands on Aida 18 (depending on desired thickness of stitches), and one strand on Hardanger 22.

When blending different colored strands, use one strand of each floss color indicated to achieve the blend.

For Backstitching, use one strand on all fabrics. When completing a French Knot, use two strands and one wrap on all fabrics.

Preparing Fabric

Cut fabric at least 3" larger on all sides than finished design size to ensure space for desired assembly. Check instructions for specific fabric allowances.

To prevent fraying, machine-zigzag or whipstitch edges or apply liquid fray preventer.

Needles for Cross Stitch

Needles should slip easily through fabric holes without piercing fabric threads. For fabric with 11 or fewer threads per inch, use a tapestry needle size 24; for 14 threads per inch, use a tapestry needle size 24 or 26; for 18 or more threads per inch, use a tapestry needle size 26.

Never leave needle in design area of fabric. It may leave rust or a permanent impression on fabric.

Floss

For each graphed piece there is a color code. Numbers and color names on this code represent DMC brand of floss. Use 18" lengths of floss. For best coverage, separate strands. Dampen with wet sponge. Then put together number of strands required.

Several pieces in this book apply the technique of blending strands. Combine one strand of each floss color indicated to achieve the blend.

Centering the Design

Fold fabric in half horizontally, then vertically. Place a pin at fold point to mark center. Locate center of design as indicated by arrows centered left and bottom on each graph. Begin stitching at center of graph and fabric.

Securing the Floss

Insert needle up from underside of fabric at starting point. Hold 1" of floss behind fabric and stitch over it, securing with the first few stitches. To finish thread, run under four or more stitches on back of design. Never knot floss, unless working on clothing.

Another method of securing floss is the waste knot. Knot floss and insert needle from the right side of fabric about 1" from design area. Work several stitches over floss to secure. Cut off knot later.

Carrying Floss

To carry floss, weave floss under previously worked stitches on back. Do not carry thread across any fabric that is not or will not be stitched. Loose threads, especially those that are dark, will show through the fabric.

Cleaning Completed Work

When stitching is complete, soak fabric in cold water with a mild soap for five to 10 minutes. Rinse well and roll in a towel to remove excess water. Do not wring. Place work face down on a dry towel and iron on warm setting until fabric is dry.

Cross Stitch

Stitches are done in a row or, if necessary, one at a time in an area.

(continued on page 126)

All of the friends sat quietly and watched as the sun dazzled them and said goodnight...

In search of my mother's garden I found my own

The birds
are almost as much a part
of the tree as its blossoms...
They come
and give it voice

Stars fade,
The sun appears
Gardening Angels
gather here

Poor indeed is the garden in which birds find no home.

Photograph on page 7.
Code and sample information begin on page 18.

Top

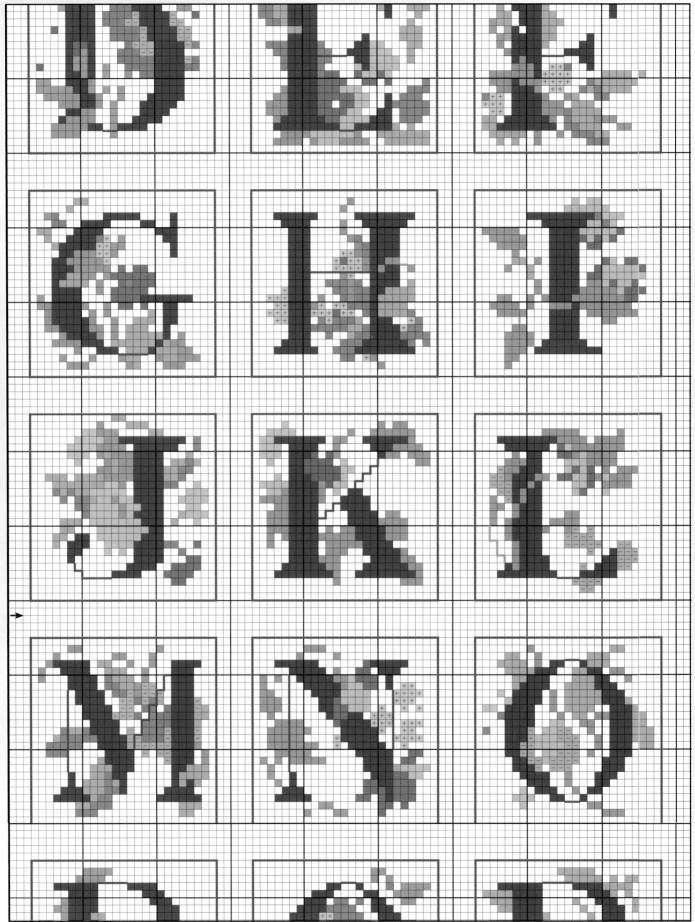

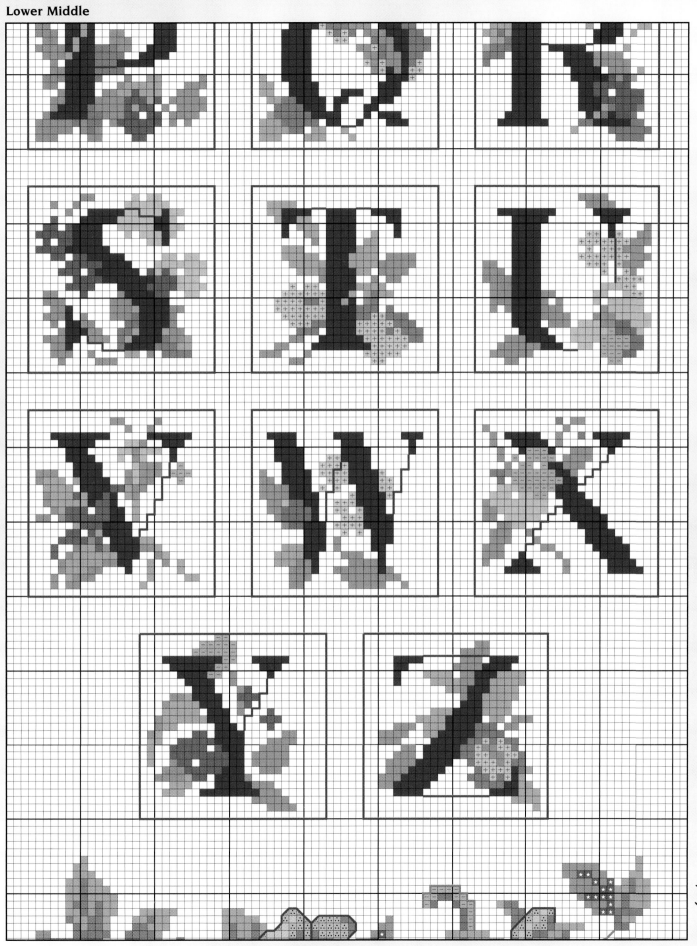

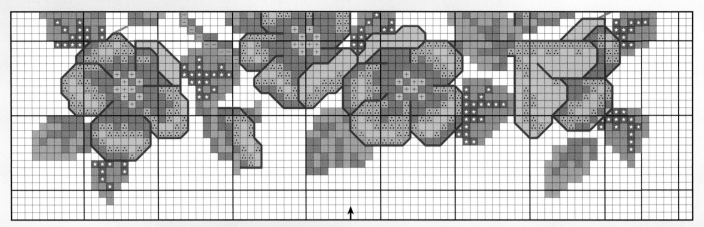

Bottom

Sample Information

The Garden Sampler sample was stitched on platinum Cashel linen 28 over two threads. The finished design size is 6¼" x 27⅛". The fabric was cut 13" x 34".

Stitch Count: 88 x 380

Other Fabrics	Finished Size
Aida 11	8" x 34½"
Aida 18	4⅞" x 21⅛"
Hardanger 22	4" x 17¼"

Anchor   DMC

Step 1: Cross Stitch (2 strands)

Anchor		DMC	
4146		754	Peach–lt.
8		761	Salmon–lt.
9		760	Salmon
11		3328	Salmon–dk.
69		3687	Mauve
869		3743	Antique Violet–vy. lt.
871		3041	Antique Violet–med.
343		3752	Antique Blue–vy. lt.
921		931	Antique Blue–med.
851		924	Slate Green–vy. dk.
842		3013	Khaki Green–lt.
844		3012	Khaki Green–med.
876		502	Blue Green
879		500	Blue Green–vy. dk.

Step 2: Backstitch (1 strand)

Anchor		DMC	
897		221	Shell Pink–vy. dk.
871		3041	Antique Violet–med.
921		931	Antique Blue–med.
844		3012	Khaki Green–med.
876		502	Blue Green
879		500	Blue Green–vy. dk. (2 strands)

Sunset

To fill the hour, that is happiness.

Photograph on page 8.

Sample Information

The sample was stitched on antique white Cashel linen 28 over two threads. The finished design size is 6⅞" x 4½". The fabric was cut 13" x 11".

Stitch Count: 96 x 63

Other Fabrics	Finished Size
Aida 11	8¾" x 5¾"
Aida 18	5⅜" x 3½"
Hardanger 22	4⅜" x 2⅞"

Anchor   DMC

Step 1: Cross Stitch (2 strands)

Anchor		DMC	
1			White
300		745	Yellow–lt. pale
881		945	Peach Beige
882		3773	Pecan–vy. lt.
271		3713	Salmon–vy. lt.
9		760	Salmon
271		3713	Salmon–vy. lt. (1 strand)
9		760	Salmon (1 strand)
10		3712	Salmon–med.
76		961	Wild Rose–dk.
42		309	Rose–deep
43		815	Garnet–med.
159		3325	Baby Blue–lt.
921		931	Antique Blue–med.
159		3325	Baby Blue–lt. (1 strand)
921		931	Antique Blue–med. (1 strand)
921		931	Antique Blue–med. (1 strand)
816		3750	Antique Blue–vy. dk. (1 strand)
816		3750	Antique Blue–vy. dk.
816		3750	Antique Blue–vy. dk. (1 strand)
1039		3810	Turquoise–dk. (1 strand)
158		747	Sky Blue–vy. lt.
185		964	Seagreen–lt.
167		3766	Peacock Blue–lt.
1039		3810	Turquoise–dk.

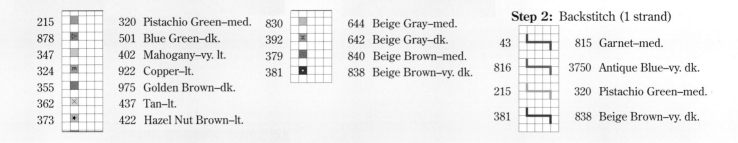

	215			320 Pistachio Green–med.		830			644 Beige Gray–med.
	878			501 Blue Green–dk.		392			642 Beige Gray–dk.
	347			402 Mahogany–vy. lt.		379			840 Beige Brown–med.
	324			922 Copper–lt.		381			838 Beige Brown–vy. dk.
	355			975 Golden Brown–dk.					
	362			437 Tan–lt.					
	373			422 Hazel Nut Brown–lt.					

Step 2: Backstitch (1 strand)

43		815 Garnet–med.
816		3750 Antique Blue–vy. dk.
215		320 Pistachio Green–med.
381		838 Beige Brown–vy. dk.

Top

Roses

A garden grows with love...

Photograph on page 9.

Sample Information

The sample was stitched on antique white Cashel linen 28 over two threads. The finished design size is 7⅝" x 7¾". The fabric was cut 14" x 14".

Stitch Count: 106 x 108

Other Fabrics	Finished Size
Aida 11	9⅝" x 9⅞"
Aida 18	5⅞" x 6"
Hardanger 22	4⅞" x 4⅞"

Anchor   DMC

Step 1: Cross Stitch (2 strands)

Anchor		DMC	
926	✗		Ecru
926			Ecru (1 strand)
6		3824	Apricot–lt. (1 strand)
386	○	746	Off White
300		745	Yellow–lt. pale
301	E	744	Yellow–pale
301		744	Yellow–pale (1 strand)
307		783	Christmas Gold (1 strand)
307		783	Christmas Gold (1 strand)
970		3726	Antique Mauve–dk. (1 strand)
6	N	3824	Apricot–lt.
8		353	Peach
10	△	352	Coral–lt.
10		352	Coral–lt. (1 strand)
35	H	3801	Christmas Red–lt. (1 strand)
11		351	Coral
13		349	Coral–dk.
35	⊡	3801	Christmas Red–lt.
47	✦	321	Christmas Red
47		321	Christmas Red (1 strand)
72		902	Garnet–vy. dk. (1 strand)
48	·	818	Baby Pink
9	–	760	Salmon
25	◇	3326	Rose–lt.
75	M	962	Wild Rose–med.
76		3731	Dusty Rose–med.
970		3726	Antique Mauve–dk.
72	◉	902	Garnet–vy. dk.
896		3721	Shell Pink–dk.
897	S	221	Shell Pink–vy. dk.
265		3348	Yellow Green–lt.
844		3012	Khaki Green–med.
846		3051	Green Gray–dk.
879		500	Blue Green–vy. dk.
307		977	Golden Brown–lt.

Left

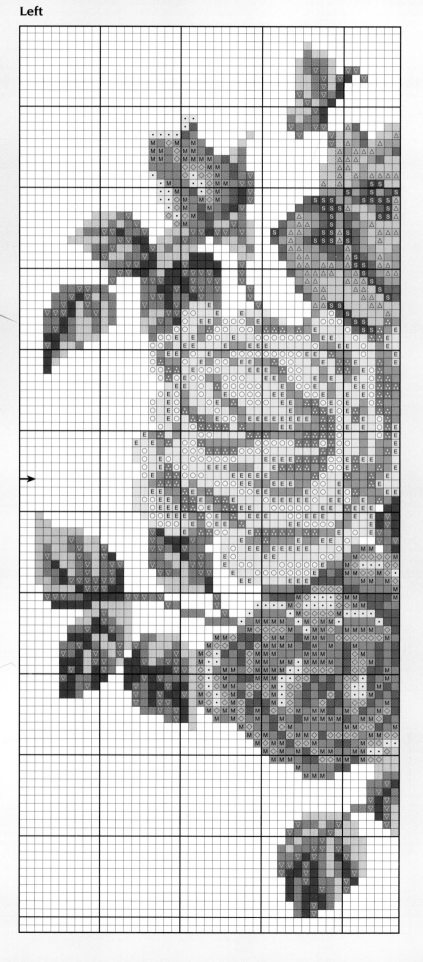

Photograph on page 10.
Code and sample information on page 24.

Top Left

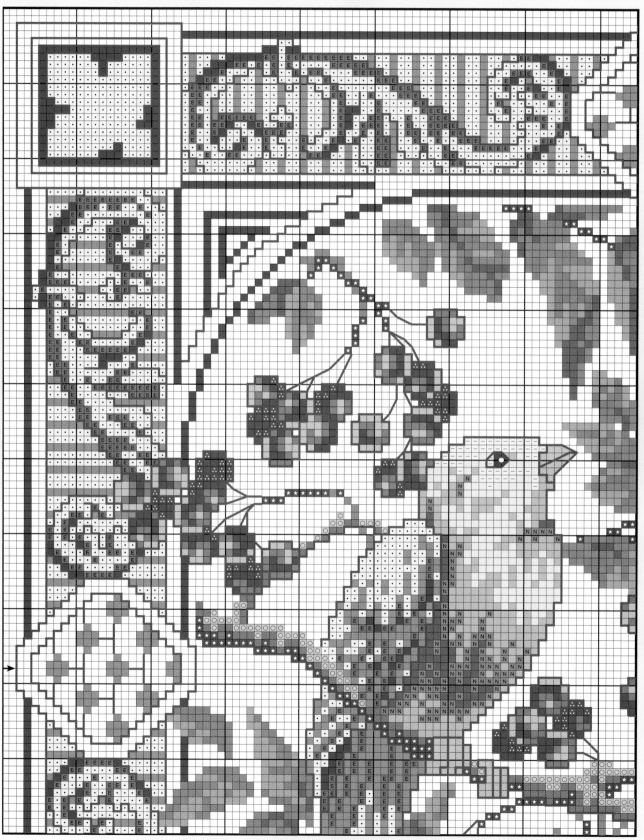

Bottom Left

Sample Information

The Birds & Berries sample was stitched on antique white Cashel linen 28 over two threads. The finished design size is 12¼" x 12¼". The fabric was cut 19" x 19".

Stitch Count: 172 x 172

Other Fabrics	Finished Size
Aida 11	15⅝" x 15⅝"
Aida 18	9½" x 9½"
Hardanger 22	7⅞" x 7⅞"

Anchor	DMC

Step 1: Cross Stitch (2 strands)

Anchor		DMC	
386		746	Off White
886		677	Old Gold–vy. lt.
887		3046	Yellow Beige–med.
373	N	3045	Yellow Beige–dk.
881		945	Peach Beige
347		402	Mahogany–vy. lt.
8		353	Peach (1 strand)
10		352	Coral–lt. (1 strand)

Anchor		DMC	
10		352	Coral–lt. (1 strand)
11		350	Coral–med. (1 strand)
11		350	Coral–med. (1 strand)
19		817	Coral Red–vy. dk. (1 strand)
20		498	Christmas Red– dk.
851		924	Slate Green–vy. dk.
842		3013	Khaki Green–lt.
844		3012	Khaki Green–med.
861		3363	Pine Green–med. (1 strand)
862		520	Fern Green–dk. (1 strand)
362	◌	437	Tan–lt.
309		435	Brown–vy. lt.
371	✶	433	Brown–med.
387	·	822	Beige Gray–lt.
956		613	Drab Brown–lt. (1 strand)
832		612	Drab Brown–med. (1 strand)
898	E	611	Drab Brown–dk.
898		611	Drab Brown–dk. (1 strand)
905		3031	Mocha Brown–vy. dk. (1 strand)
944		869	Hazel Nut Brown–vy. dk.
380		839	Beige Brown–dk.

Step 2: Backstitch (1 strand)

Anchor		DMC	
371		433	Brown–med. (cherry stems)

Anchor		DMC	
905		3031	Mocha Brown–vy. dk. (branches)
380		839	Beige Brown–dk. (all else)

Step 3: French Knot (1 strand)

Anchor		DMC	
387	○	822	Beige Gray–lt.

Bottom Right

Ripened Fruit

"Take time for all things."—Benjamin Franklin

Photograph on page 12.

Anchor   **DMC**

Step 1: Cross Stitch (2 strands)

Anchor	DMC	
926		Ecru
301	744	Yellow–pale
306	3820	Straw–dk.
891	676	Old Gold–lt.
307	977	Golden Brown–lt.
318	3776	Mahogany–lt.
9	760	Salmon
10	351	Coral
11	350	Coral–med.
13	349	Coral–dk.
19	817	Coral Red–vy. dk.
20	498	Christmas Red–dk.
897	221	Shell Pink–vy. dk.
72	902	Garnet–vy. dk.

Anchor	DMC	
159	3325	Baby Blue–lt.
130	799	Delft–med.
922	930	Antique Blue–dk.
121	793	Cornflower Blue–med.
940	792	Cornflower Blue–dk.
941	791	Cornflower Blue–vy. dk.
104	210	Lavender–med.
119	333	Blue Violet–vy. dk.
101	550	Violet–vy. dk.
266	471	Avocado Green–vy. dk.
215	320	Pistachio Green–med.
878	501	Blue Green–dk.
862	934	Black Avocado Green
363	436	Tan
393	3790	Beige Gray–ultra vy. dk.
373	422	Hazel Nut Brown–lt.

Sample Information

The Cherries sample was stitched on cream Brittany 28 over two threads. The finished design size is 2½" x 3⅛". The fabric was cut 9" x 10". Graph is on page 26.

Stitch Count: 35 x 43

Other Fabrics	Finished Size
Aida 11	3⅛" x 4"
Aida 18	2" x 2⅜"
Hardanger 22	1⅝" x 2"

Cherries

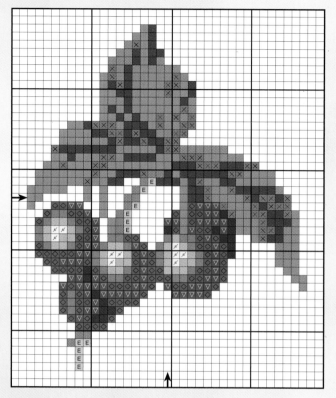

Sample Information

The Grapes sample was stitched on cream Brittany 28 over two threads. The finished design size is 2½" x 3¼". The fabric was cut 9" x 10". Use code on page 25.

Stitch Count: 35 x 46

Other Fabrics	Finished Size
Aida 11	3⅛" x 4⅛"
Aida 18	2" x 2½"
Hardanger 22	1⅝" x 2⅛"

Sample Information

The Peaches sample was stitched on cream Brittany 28 over two threads. The finished design size is 2⅝" x 2¾". The fabric was cut 9" x 10". Use code on page 25.

Stitch Count: 36 x 38

Other Fabrics	Finished Size
Aida 11	3¼" x 3½"
Aida 18	2" x 2⅛"
Hardanger 22	1⅝" x 1¾"

Grapes

Peaches

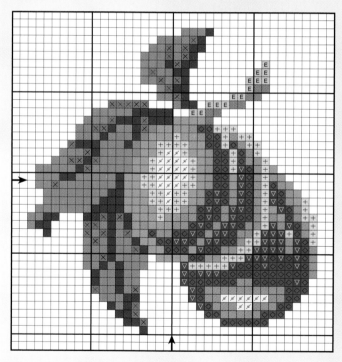

Sample Information

The Plums sample was stitched on cream Brittany 28 over two threads. The finished design size is 2⅞" x 3¾". The fabric was cut 9" x 10". Use code on page 25.

Stitch Count: 40 x 53

Other Fabrics	**Finished Size**
Aida 11	3⅝" x 4¾"
Aida 18	2¼" x 3"
Hardanger 22	1⅞" x 2⅜"

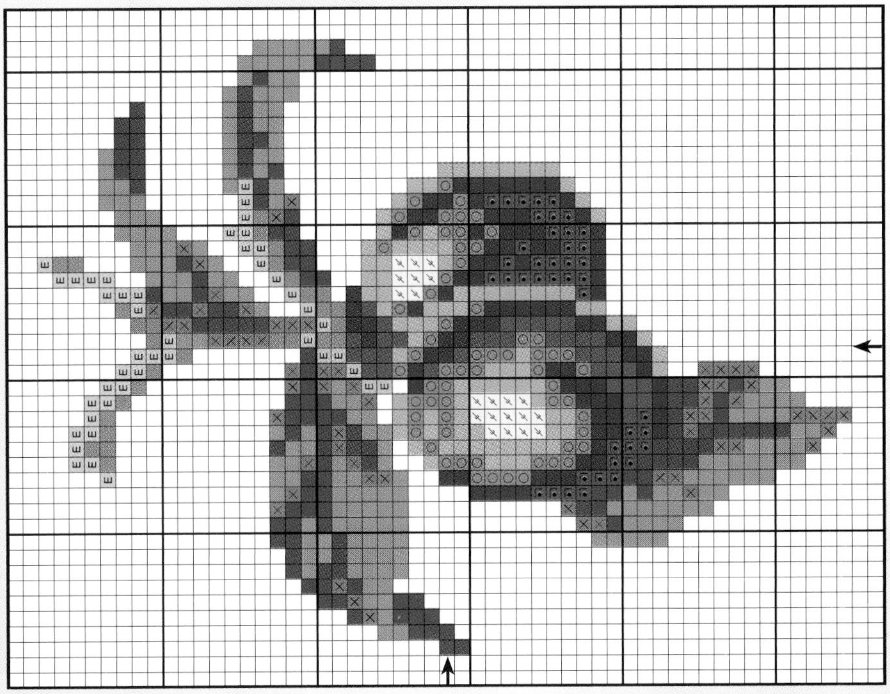

Plums Top

Sample Information

The Pears sample was stitched on cream Brittany 28 over two threads. The finished design size is 2¼" x 2¾". The fabric was cut 9" x 10". Use code on page 25.

Stitch Count: 31 x 38

Other Fabrics	**Finished Size**
Aida 11	2⅞" x 3½"
Aida 18	1¾" x 2⅛"
Hardanger 22	1⅜" x 1¾"

Pears

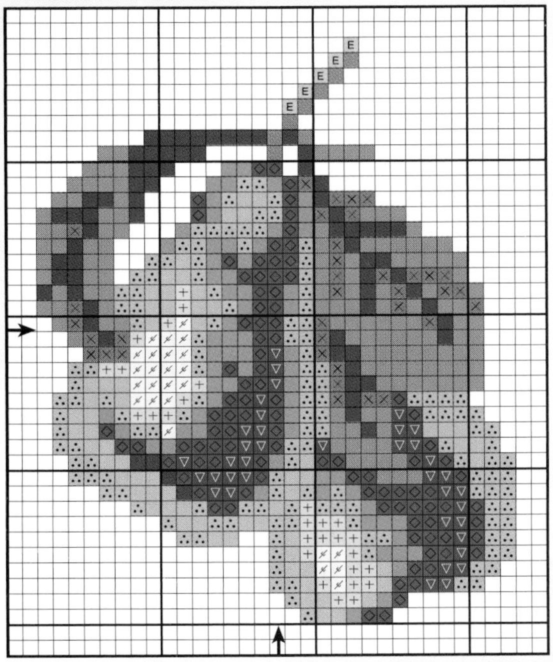

Sample Information

The Apples sample was stitched on cream Brittany 28 over two threads. The finished design size is 2¾" x 3⅛". The fabric was cut 9" x 10". Use code on page 25.

Stitch Count: 39 x 44

Other Fabrics	**Finished Size**
Aida 11	3½" x 4"
Aida 18	2⅛" x 2½"
Hardanger 22	1¾" x 2"

Apples

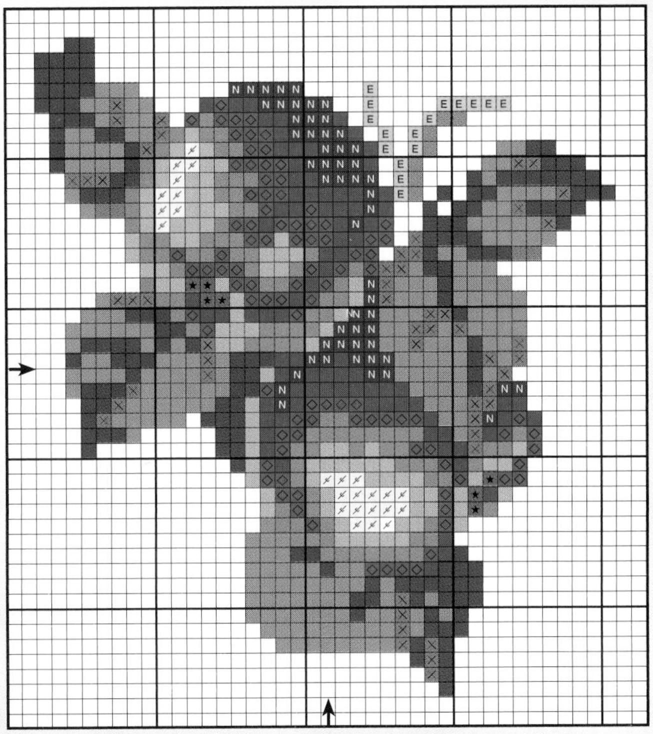

Sample Information

The Verse sample was stitched on cream Brittany 28 over two threads. The finished design size is 2⅞" x 3⅝". The fabric was cut 9" x 10". Use code on page 25.

Stitch Count: 40 x 50

Other Fabrics	**Finished Size**
Aida 11	3⅝" x 4½"
Aida 18	2¼" x 2¾"
Hardanger 22	1⅞" x 2¼"

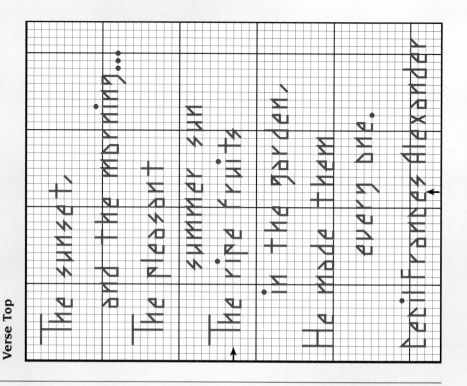

Verse Top

Angel Cottage

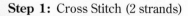

Be not forgetful to entertain strangers, for thereby some have entertained angels...

Photograph on page 13.

Sample Information

The sample was stitched on white Glasgow linen 28 over two threads. The finished design size is 11⅜" x 7⅛". The fabric was cut 18" x 14".

Stitch Count: 160 x 100

Other Fabrics	**Finished Size**
Aida 11	14½" x 9⅛"
Aida 18	8⅞" x 5½"
Hardanger 22	7¼" x 4½"

Step 1: Cross Stitch (2 strands)

Anchor	**DMC**	
1		White
926		Ecru
886	677	Old Gold–vy. lt.
886	677	Old Gold–vy. lt. (1 strand)
891	676	Old Gold–lt. (1 strand)
891	676	Old Gold–lt. (1 strand)
304	3045	Yellow Beige–dk. (1 strand)
304	3045	Yellow Beige–dk.
304	3045	Yellow Beige–dk. (1 strand)
266	471	Avocado Green–vy. lt. (1 strand)
366	951	Peach Pecan–lt.
881	945	Peach Beige
347	402	Mahogany–vy. lt.
338	3776	Mahogany–lt.
9	760	Salmon
11	3328	Salmon–dk.
13	347	Salmon–vy. dk.
897	221	Shell Pink–vy. dk.
25	3326	Rose–lt.
25	3326	Rose–lt. (1 strand)
76	961	Wild Rose–dk. (1 strand)
76	961	Wild Rose–dk.
76	961	Wild Rose–dk. (1 strand)
871	3041	Antique Violet–med. (1 strand)
22	816	Garnet
1		White (1 strand)
158	775	Baby Blue–vy. lt. (1 strand)
158	775	Baby Blue–vy. lt.
158	775	Baby Blue–vy. lt. (1 strand)
159	3325	Baby Blue–lt. (1 strand)
159	3325	Baby Blue–lt.
920	932	Antique Blue–lt.
264	772	Pine Green–lt.
266	471	Avocado Green–vy. lt.
875	503	Blue Green–med.
875	503	Blue Green–med. (1 strand)
379	840	Beige Brown–med. (1 strand)
861	3363	Pine Green–med.
840	3768	Slate Green–dk.
840	3768	Slate Green–dk. (1 strand)
380	839	Beige Brown–dk. (1 strand)

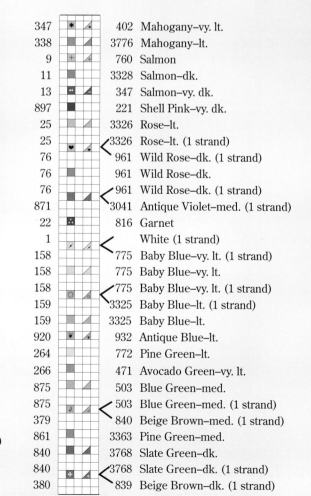

926	Ecru (1 strand)	830		644	Beige Gray–med.			871		3041	Antique Violet–med.
362	437 Tan–lt. (1 strand)	392		642	Beige Gray–dk.			22		816	Garnet
362	437 Tan–lt. (1 strand)	379		840	Beige Brown–med.						
379	840 Beige Brown (1 strand)	380		839	Beige Brown–dk.						

Left

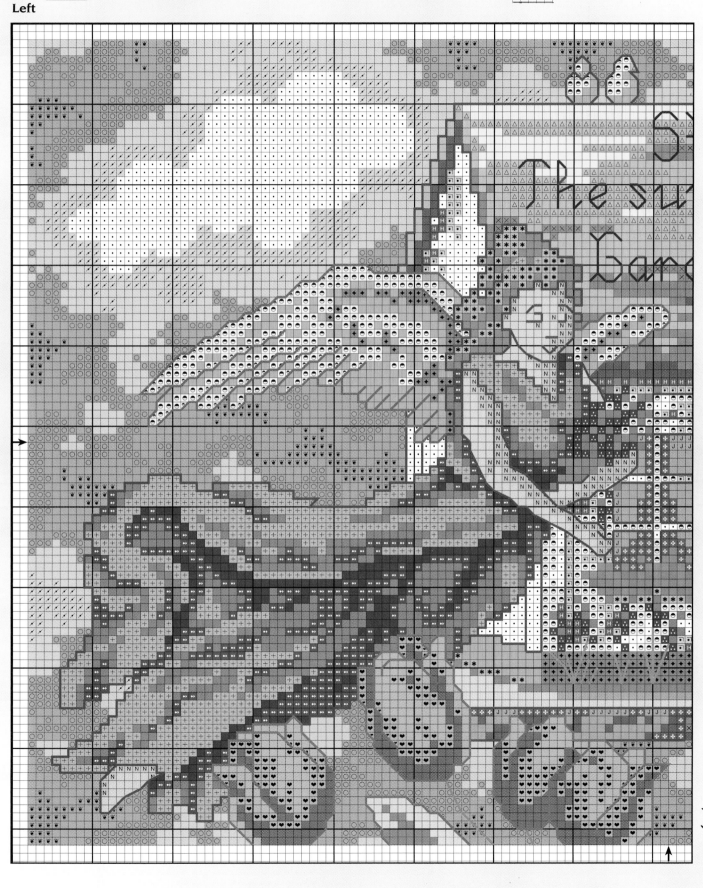

	840	3768 Slate Green–dk.
	379	840 Beige Brown–med.
	380	839 Beige Brown–dk.

| | 382 | 3371 Black Brown (2 strands) |

Step 3: Long Stitch (2 strands)

| | 266 | 471 Avocado Green–vy. lt. |

Step 4: French Knot (1 strand)

| | 382 | 3371 Black Brown (2 strands) |

"Nothing happens to any man that he is not formed by nature to bear."
—Marcus Aurelius

Photograph on page 14.

Anchor	DMC	

Step 1: Cross Stitch (2 strands)

Anchor		DMC	
1	+		White
386	·	746	Off White
300		745	Yellow–lt. pale
305	×	3822	Straw–lt.
891		676	Old Gold–lt.
890		729	Old Gold–med.
890		729	Old Gold–med. (1 strand)
871		3041	Antique Violet–med. (1 strand)
871		3041	Antique Violet–med. (1 strand)
338		3776	Mahogany–lt. (1 strand)
8		761	Salmon–lt.
9		3712	Salmon–med. (1 strand)
10		352	Coral–lt. (1 strand)

Anchor		DMC	
9		3712	Salmon–med. (1 strand)
11		350	Coral–med. (1 strand)
13	N	349	Coral–dk.
47		321	Christmas Red (1 strand)
59		304	Christmas Red–med. (1 strand)
43		815	Garnet–med.
72		902	Garnet–vy. dk.
118		340	Blue Violet–med.
940		3807	Cornflower Blue
149		311	Navy Blue–med.
851		924	Slate Green–vy. dk.
874		834	Olive Green–vy. lt.
264		472	Avocado Green–ultra lt.
266	◎	471	Avocado Green–vy. lt.
844	★	3012	Khaki Green–med.

Anchor		DMC	
844		3012	Khaki Green–med. (1 strand)
878		501	Blue Green–dk. (1 strand)
846		3051	Green Gray–dk.
843		3364	Pine Green
861		3363	Pine Green–med.
878	∨	501	Blue Green–dk.
878	E	501	Blue Green–dk. (1 strand)
375		420	Hazel Nut Brown–dk. (1 strand)
879		500	Blue Green–vy. dk.
373		422	Hazel Nut Brown–lt.
375		420	Hazel Nut Brown–dk.
378		841	Beige Brown–lt.
379		840	Beige Brown–med.
380	H	839	Beige Brown–dk.

Step 2: Backstitch (1 strand)

Anchor		DMC	
118		340	Blue Violet–med.
940		3807	Cornflower Blue

Sample Information

The sample was stitched on rue green Belfast linen 32 over two threads. The finished design size for each is 4½" x 4½". The fabric for each was cut 11" x 11".

Stitch Count for each: 72 x 72

Other Fabrics	Finished Size
Aida 11	6½" x 6½"
Aida 14	5⅛" x 5⅛"
Aida 18	4" x 4"
Hardanger 22	3¼" x 3¼"

Apples

Verse Top

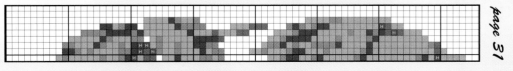

Verse Bottom

Pears

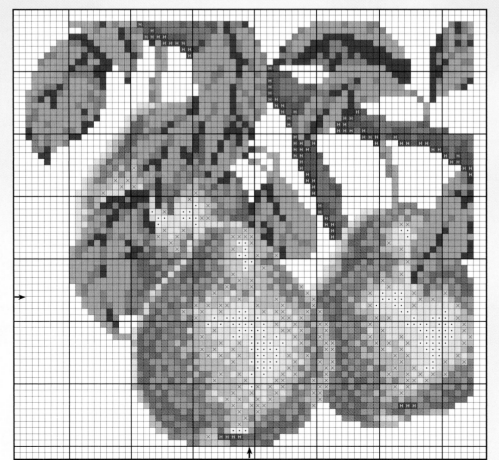

There's nothing half so sweet in life as love's young dream

"Imagination is more important than knowledge."—Albert Einstein

Photograph on page 33.

Anchor   DMC

Step 1: Cross Stitch (2 strands)

386	746	Off White
891	676	Old Gold–lt.
271	3713	Salmon–vy. lt.
894	223	Shell Pink–med.
871	3041	Antique Violet–med.
872	3740	Antique Violet–dk.
872	3740	Antique Violet–dk. (1 strand)
150	823	Navy Blue–dk. (1 strand)
117	341	Blue Violet–lt.
118	340	Blue Violet–med.
859	3052	Green Gray–med.
862	935	Avocado Green–dk.
309	435	Brown–vy. lt.
380	839	Beige Brown–dk.
900	648	Beaver Gray–lt.

Step 2: Backstitch (1 strand)

872	3740	Antique Violet–dk.
309	435	Brown–vy. lt.
380	839	Beige Brown–dk.

Step 3: Long Stitch (1 strand)

309	435	Brown–vy. lt. (Side panels on door)

Step 4: French Knot (1 strand)

872	3740	Antique Violet–dk.

Sample Information

The Window sample was stitched on pink Royal Cherub 28 over two threads. The finished design size is 3⅞" x 6⅛". The fabric was cut 10" x 13".

Stitch Count: 54 x 85

Other Fabrics	Finished Size
Aida 11	4⅞" x 7¾"
Aida 18	3" x 4¾"
Hardanger 22	2½" x 3⅞"

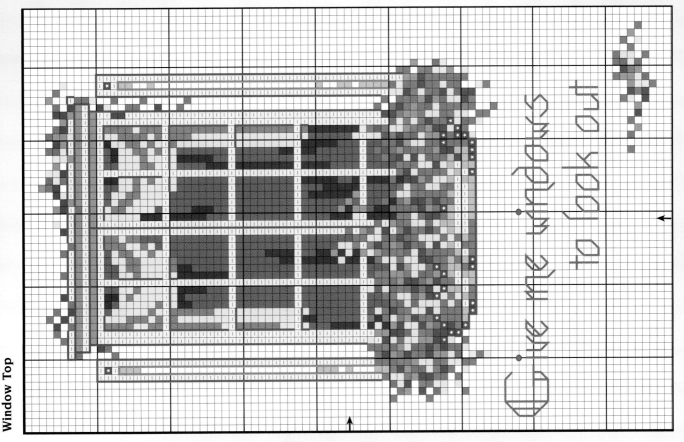

Window Top

Sample Information

The Door sample was stitched on white pink Royal Cherub 28 over two threads. The finished design size is 4⅞" x 7⅛". The fabric was cut 11" x 14". Use code on page 39.

Stitch Count: 116 x 140

Other Fabrics	Finished Size
Aida 11	6¼" x 9"
Aida 18	3⅞" x 5½"
Hardanger 22	3⅛" x 4½"

Door

Heartstrings are the bow that ties the gift of friendship.

Photograph on page 34.

Left

Sample Information

The sample was stitched on mushroom Lugana 25 over two threads. The finished design size is 7" x 8". The fabric was cut 13" x 14".

Stitch Count: 88 x 100

Other Fabrics	Finished Size
Aida 11	8" x 9⅛"
Aida 14	6¼" x 7⅛"
Aida 18	4⅞" x 5½"
Hardanger 22	4" x 4½"

Anchor		DMC	

Step 1: Cross Stitch (2 strands)

Anchor		DMC	
1	–		White
386		746	Off White
300	○	745	Yellow–lt.pale
891		676	Old Gold–lt.
366		951	Peach Pecan–lt.
881	×	945	Peach Beige
868		758	Terra Cotta–lt.
323		722	Orange Spice–lt.
117		341	Blue Violet–lt.
128		800	Delft–pale
121	E	794	Cornflower Blue–lt.
940		793	Cornflower Blue–med.
842		3013	Khaki Green–lt.
859		523	Fern Green–lt.
846		3052	Green Gray–med.
373	M	422	Hazel Nut Brown–lt.
8581		647	Beaver Gray–med.
905	✶	646	Beaver Gray–dk.
401		844	Beaver Gray–ultra dk.

Step 2: Backstitch (1 strand)

Anchor		DMC	
922		930	Antique Blue–dk.
380		839	Beige Brown–dk.
401		844	Beaver Gray–ultra dk.

Step 3: Long Stitch (1 strand)

Anchor		DMC	
922		930	Antique Blue–dk.
842		3013	Khaki Green–lt.

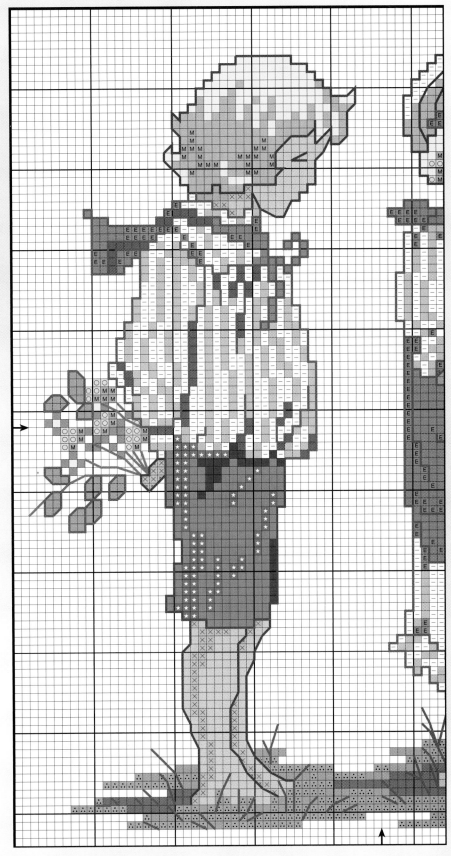

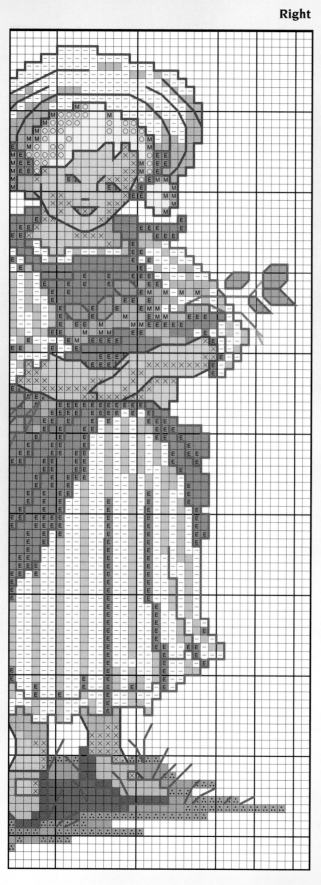

The sample was stitched on dawn gray Annabelle 28 over two threads. The finished design size is 7¼" x 10⅞". The fabric was cut 14" x 17".

Stitch Count: 101 x 152

Other Fabrics	Finished Size
Aida 11	9⅛" x 13⅞"
Aida 18	5⅝" x 8½"
Hardanger 22	4⅝" x 6⅞"

Middle

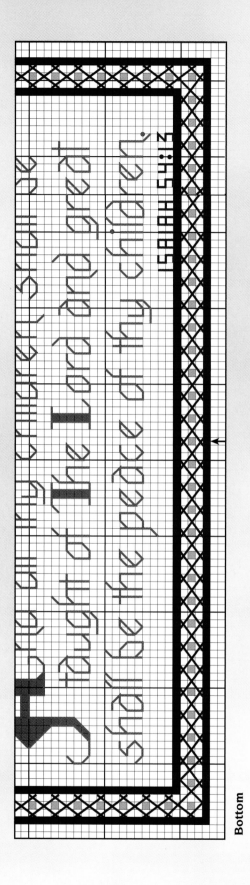

Bottom

Anchor   **DMC**

Step 1: Cross Stitch (2 strands)

Anchor	Symbol	DMC	Color
1			White
886		677	Old Gold–vy. lt.
891		676	Old Gold–lt.
890		729	Old Gold–med.
890		729	Old Gold–med. (1 strand)
871		3041	Antique Violet–med. (1 strand)
366		951	Peach Pecan–lt.
881		945	Peach Beige
8		761	Salmon–lt.
9		760	Salmon
894		223	Shell Pink–med.
970		3726	Antique Mauve–dk.
169		806	Peacock Blue–dk.
149		311	Navy Blue–med.
149		311	Navy Blue–med. (1 strand)
844		3012	Khaki Green–med. (1 strand)
851		924	Slate Green–vy. dk.
928		3811	Turquoise–vy. lt. (1 strand)
876		502	Blue Green (1 strand)
876		502	Blue Green
879		500	Blue Green–vy. dk.
279		734	Olive Green–lt.
279		734	Olive Green–lt. (1 strand)
845		3011	Khaki Green–dk. (1 strand)
842		3013	Khaki Green–lt.
844		3012	Khaki Green–med.
845		3011	Khaki Green–dk.
861		3362	Pine Green–dk.
862		934	Black Avocado Green
307		977	Golden Brown–lt.
309		435	Brown–vy. lt.
371		433	Brown–med.
378		841	Beige Brown–lt.
393		3790	Beige Gray–ultra vy. dk.
905		3031	Mocha Brown–vy. dk.

Step 2: Backstitch (1 strand)

Anchor	DMC	Color
149	311	Navy Blue–med.
851	924	Slate Green–vy. dk.
371	433	Brown–med. (branches) (2 strands)
371	433	Brown–med.
393	3790	Beige Gray–ultra vy. dk.
905	3031	Mocha Brown–vy. dk.

Step 3: French Knot (1 strand)

Anchor	DMC	Color
851	924	Slate Green–vy. dk.
905	3031	Mocha Brown–vy. dk.

They thought we were sisters...but we were closer.

Photograph on page 36.
Code and sample information begin on page 46.

Top Left

Sample Information

The sample was stitched on pewter Murano 30 over two threads. The finished design size is 8⅞" x 8¾". The fabric was cut 15" x 15".

Stitch Count: 134 x 132

Other Fabrics	Finished Size
Aida 11	12⅛" x 12"
Aida 14	9⅝" x 9⅜"
Aida 18	7½" x 7⅜"
Hardanger 22	6⅛" x 6"

Anchor		DMC	

Step 1: Cross Stitch (2 strands)

Anchor	Symbol	DMC	Color
926			Ecru
886		677	Old Gold–vy. lt.
886		677	Old Gold–vy. lt. (1 strand)
891		676	Old Gold–lt. (1 strand)
366		951	Peach Pecan–lt.
881		945	Peach Beige
868		758	Terra Cotta–lt.
271		3713	Salmon–vy. lt.
10		3712	Salmon–med.
75	K	3733	Dusty Rose–lt.
896		3721	Shell Pink–dk.
95		554	Violet–lt.
110		208	Lavender–vy. dk.
158	+	3756	Baby Blue–ultra vy. lt. (1 strand)
160		3761	Sky Blue–lt. (1 strand)
160		3761	Sky Blue–lt.
922		930	Antique Blue–dk.
779		926	Slate Green
851		924	Slate Green–vy. dk.
213		369	Pistachio Green–vy. lt.
264		472	Avocado Green–ultra lt.
266	N	3347	Yellow Green–med.
842	△	3013	Khaki Green–lt.
844	E	3012	Khaki Green–med.
860	★	3053	Green Gray
846		3051	Green Gray–dk.
861		3363	Pine Green–med.
876	H	502	Blue Green
246		319	Pistachio Green–vy. dk.
376		842	Beige Brown–vy. lt.
378		841	Beige Brown–lt.
379		840	Beige Brown–med.
380		839	Beige Brown–dk.
914		3772	Pecan–med.
936		632	Pecan–dk.
5975		356	Terra Cotta–med.
341		918	Red Copper–dk.
382		3371	Black Brown

Step 2: Backstitch (1 strand)

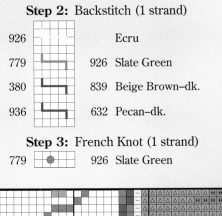

926		Ecru
779		926 Slate Green
380		839 Beige Brown–dk.
936		632 Pecan–dk.

Step 3: French Knot (1 strand)

779		926 Slate Green

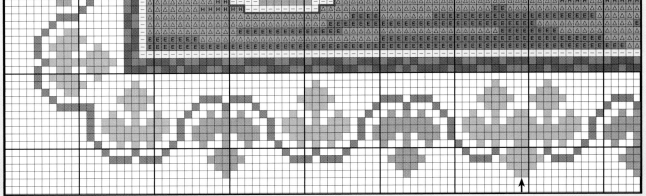

Bottom Left

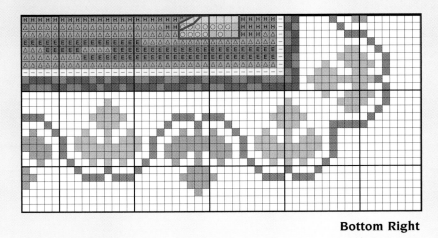

Bottom Right

Additional Verse

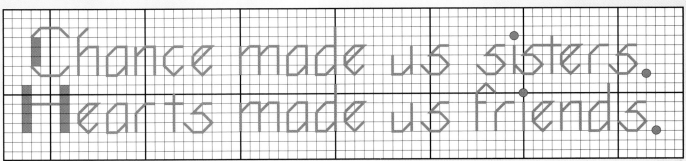

Chance made us sisters.
Hearts made us friends.

Photograph on page 37.
Code and sample information on page 50.

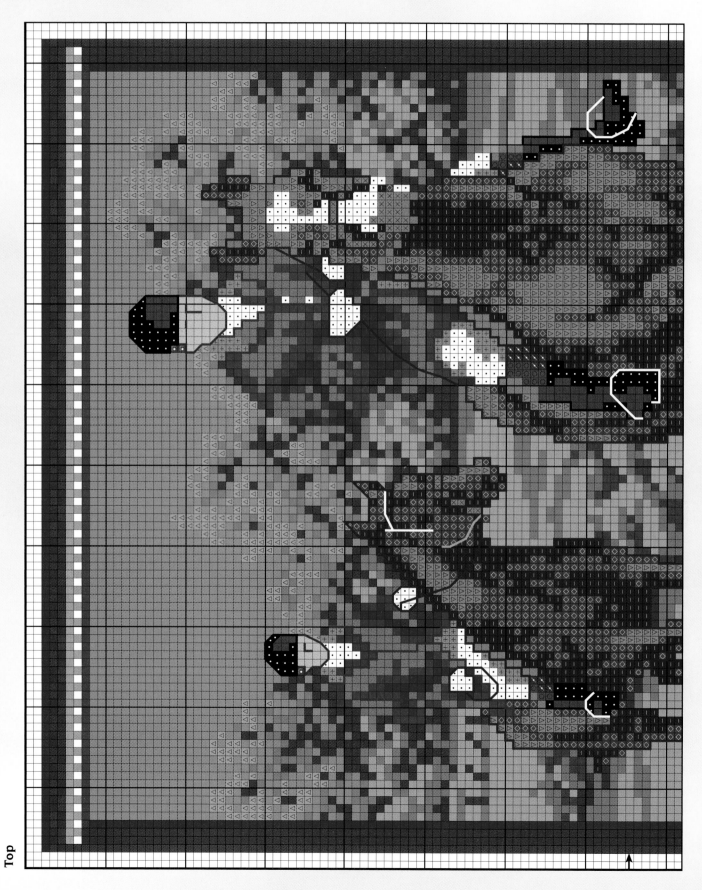

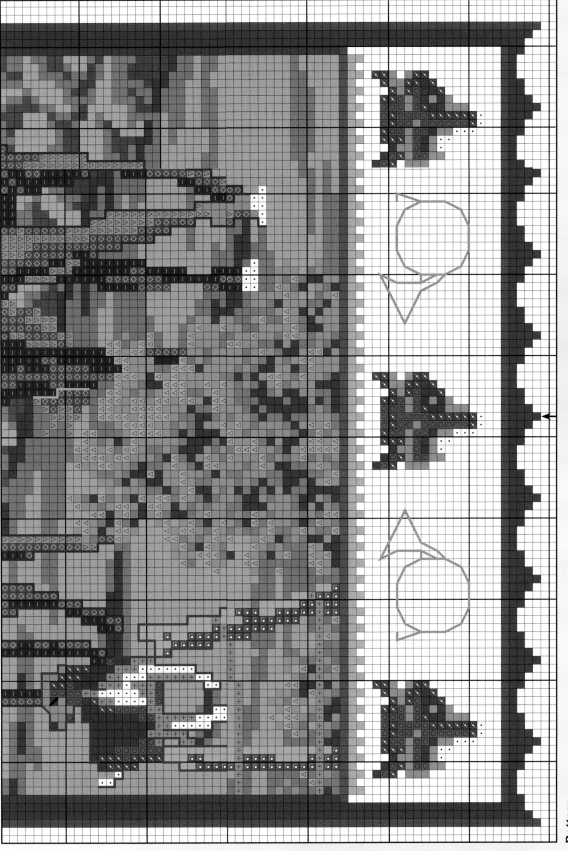

Sample Information

The sample was stitched on driftwood Dublin 25 over two threads. The finished design size is 8⅛" x 11¾". The fabric was cut 15" x 18".

Stitch Count: 101 x 147

Other Fabrics	Finished Size
Aida 11	9⅛" x 13⅜"
Aida 14	7¼" x 10½"
Aida 18	5⅝" x 8⅛"
Hardanger 22	4⅝" x 6⅝"

Anchor   DMC

Step 1: Cross Stitch (2 strands)

Anchor		DMC	
1			White
881		945	Peach Beige
11		3328	Salmon–dk.
13		347	Salmon–vy. dk.
897		221	Shell Pink–vy. dk.
130		809	Delft
816		3750	Antique Blue–vy. dk.
842		3013	Khaki Green–lt.
280		733	Olive Green–med.
859		522	Fern Green
268		937	Avocado Green–med.
878		501	Blue Green–dk.
879		500	Blue Green–vy. dk.
887		3046	Yellow Beige–med.
888		3828	Hazel Nut Brown
338		3776	Mahogany–lt.
339		920	Copper–med.
352		300	Mahogany–vy. dk.
882		407	Pecan (1 strand)
371		433	Brown–med. (1 strand)
956		613	Drab Brown–lt.
903		640	Beige Gray–vy. dk.
378		841	Beige Brown–lt.
380		839	Beige Brown–dk.
371		433	Brown–med. (1 strand)
381		938	Coffee Brown–ultra dk. (1 strand)
382		3371	Black Brown
8581		3023	Brown Gray–lt.
401		844	Beaver Gray–ultra dk.
403		310	Black

Step 2: Backstitch (1 strand)

Anchor		DMC	
1			White (2 strands) (stirrups)
1			White
897		221	Shell Pink–vy. dk.
888		3828	Hazel Nut Brown (2 strands) (horns)
381		938	Coffee Brown–ultra dk. (1 strand)
382		3371	Black Brown (2 strands) (whips)
403		310	Black

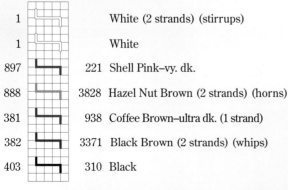

Additional Verse Top

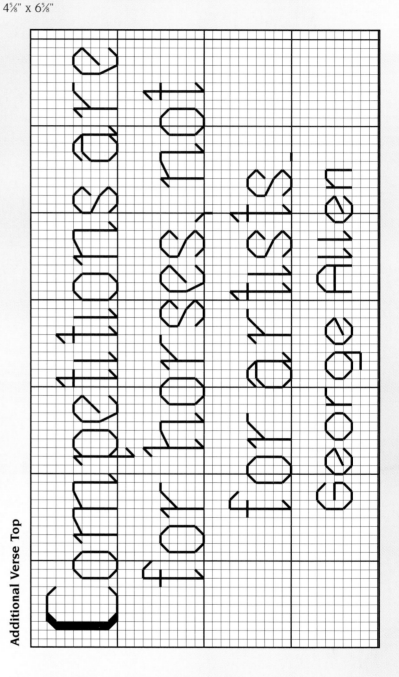

Competitions are not horses not for artists. George Allen

"Records are made to be broken."—Baseball Saying

The Game

Photograph on page 38.
Code and sample information on page 53.

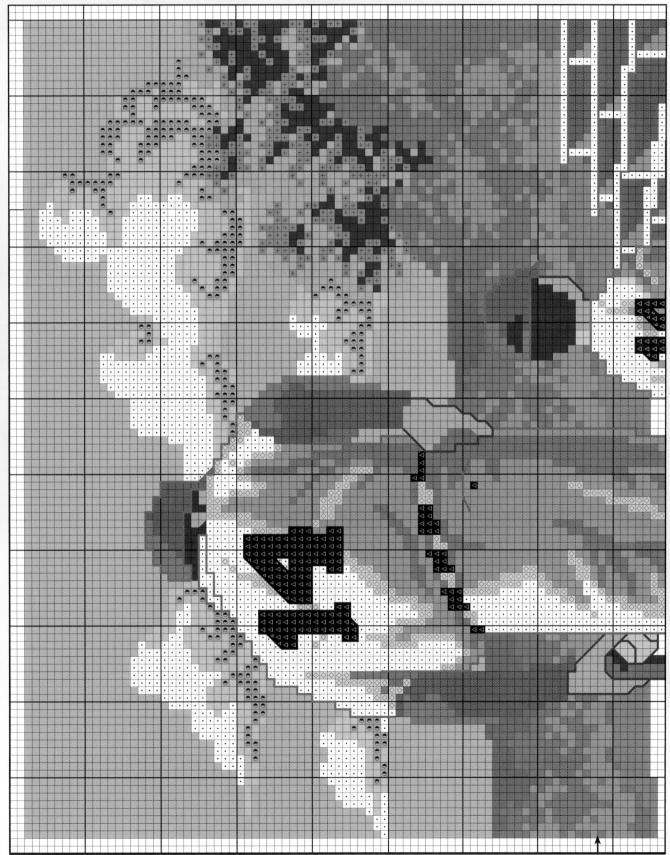

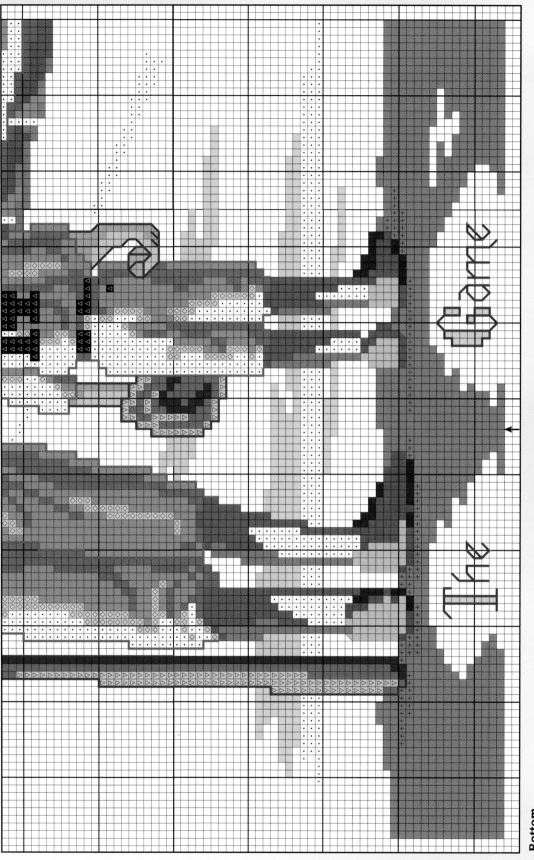

Sample Information

The sample was stitched on cream Jubilee 28 over two threads. The finished design size is 7¾" x 10⅞". The fabric was cut 14" x 17".

Stitch Count: 108 x 152

Other Fabrics	Finished Size
Aida 11	9⅞" x 13⅞"
Aida 18	6" x 8½"
Hardanger 22	4⅞" x 6⅞"

Anchor	DMC	

Step 1: Cross Stitch (2 strands)

Anchor		DMC	
1			White
891		676	Old Gold–lt.
890		729	Old Gold–med.
881		945	Peach Beige
882		3773	Pecan–vy. lt.
108		211	Lavender–lt. (1 strand)
869		3743	Antique Violet–vy. lt. (1 strand)
105		209	Lavender–dk.
870		3042	Antique Violet–lt.
871		3041	Antique Violet–med.
872		3740	Antique Violet–dk.
117		3747	Blue Violet–vy. lt.
118		341	Blue Violet–lt.
119		3746	Blue Violet–dk.
128		800	Delft–pale
121		793	Cornflower Blue–med.
928		598	Turquoise–lt.
264		472	Avocado Green–ultra lt.
844		3012	Khaki Green–med.
859		3052	Green Gray–med.
861		3363	Pine Green–med.
862		520	Fern Green–dk.
879		500	Blue Green–vy. dk.
311		3827	Golden Brown–pale
363		436	Tan
370		434	Brown–lt.
357		801	Coffee Brown–dk.
397		453	Shell Gray–lt.
399		451	Shell Gray–dk.
401		535	Ash Gray–vy. lt.
872		3740	Antique Violet–dk. (1 strand)
403		310	Black (1 strand)

Step 2: Backstitch (1 strand)

Anchor		DMC	
872		3740	Antique Violet–dk.
357		801	Coffee Brown–dk.
403		310	Black

NOTE: Optional hair colors for girl can be:
Brunette: #434 Brown–lt.
    #801 Coffee Brown–dk.

Redhead: #3776 Mahogany–lt.
    #301 Mahogany–med.

Optional Girl Player

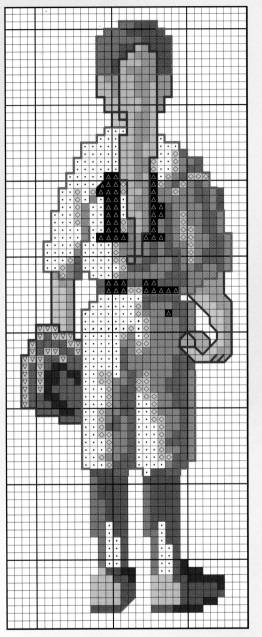

A dream is a wish your heart makes

Great things come in small pieces.

We are just as different as we can be. But dearest friends we will always be.

Joys come from simple and natural things

On with the dance!
Let joy be unconfined.

Today we should do well
to take a moment to dream
of lighthearted and sweet
beautiful things
like butterflies and daffodils
and birds that sing.

In the name of the bees and the butterflies and the trees. Amen.

Photographs on pages 54–55.

Sample Information

The sample was stitched on ice blue Annabelle 28 over two threads. The finished design size is 9¼" x 13¼". The fabric was cut 16" x 20". Brackets on graph indicate where optional stitching of verse begins.

Stitch Count: 129 x 185

Other Fabrics	Finished Size
Aida 11	11¾" x 16⅞"
Aida 18	7⅛" x 10¼"
Hardanger 22	5⅞" x 8⅜"

Anchor   DMC

Step 1: Cross Stitch (2 strands)

Anchor		DMC	
1	–		White
300	·	3823	Yellow–ultra pale
891		676	Old Gold–lt.
881		945	Peach Beige
10		352	Coral–lt.
25	△	3326	Rose–lt.
42		335	Rose
59		326	Rose–vy. dk.
85	+	3609	Plum–ultra lt.
98		553	Violet–med.
117		341	Blue Violet–lt.
117		341	Blue Violet–lt. (1 strand)
121		793	Cornflower Blue–med. (1 strand)
121		793	Cornflower Blue–med.
940	▣	792	Cornflower Blue–dk.
264		472	Avocado Green–ultra lt.
844		3012	Khaki Green–med.
924		730	Olive Green–vy. dk.
266		3347	Yellow Green–med.
859	E	3052	Green Gray–med.
861		3363	Pine Green–med.
879		500	Blue Green–vy. dk.
887	H	372	Mustard–lt.
888	N	3828	Hazel Nut Brown
1014		3830	Terra Cotta
882		3773	Pecan–vy. lt.
914		3772	Pecan–med.
942		738	Tan–vy. lt.
338		3776	Mahogany–lt.
351		400	Mahogany–dk.
357		801	Coffee Brown–dk.
8581		3022	Brown Gray–med.
403	◼	310	Black

Step 2: Backstitch (1 strand)

59		326	Rose–vy. dk.
940		792	Cornflower Blue–dk. (2 strands) (in dress)
940		792	Cornflower Blue–dk.
846		3051	Green Gray–dk.
1014		3830	Terra Cotta
357		801	Coffee Brown–dk. (2 strands) (girl's eye, eyebrow)
357		801	Coffee Brown–dk.
403		310	Black

Step 3: French Knot (1 strand)

403	●	310	Black

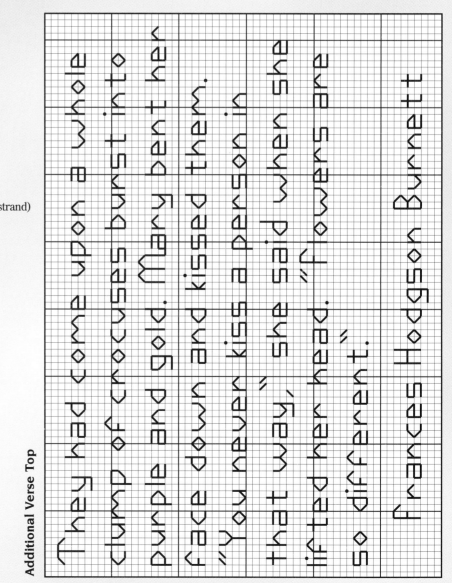

Additional Verse Top

They had come upon a whole clump of crocuses burst into purple and gold. Mary bent her face down and kissed them. "You never kiss a person in that way," she said when she lifted her head. "Flowers are so different."

Frances Hodgson Burnett

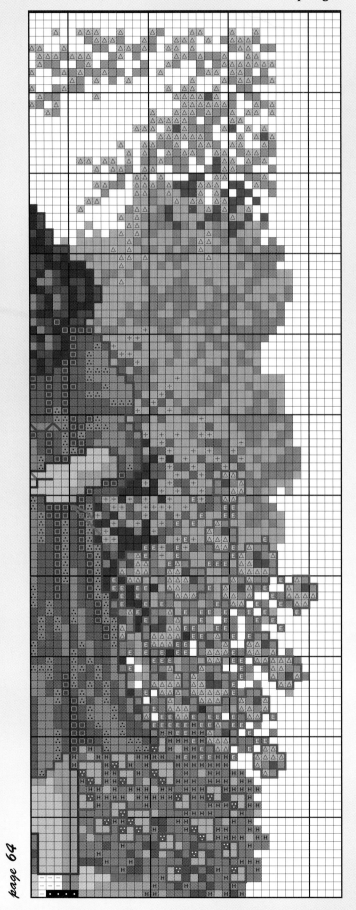

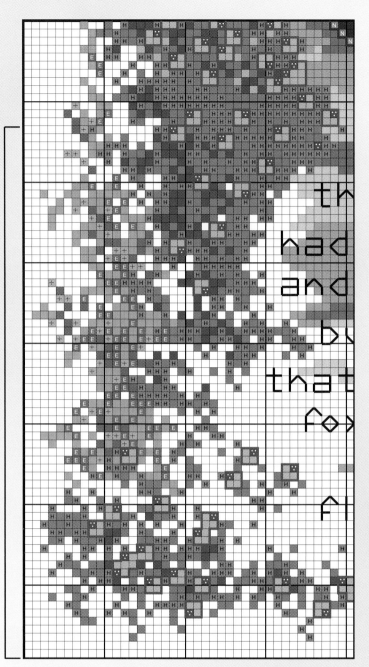

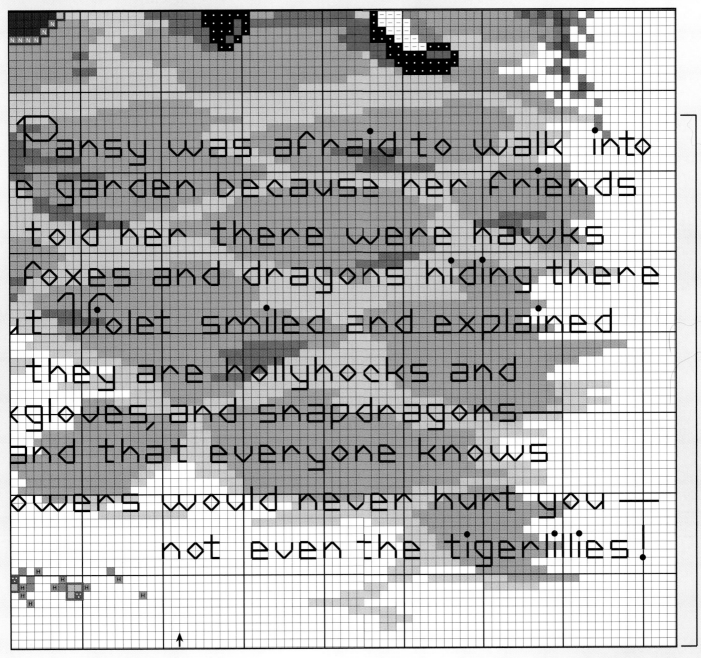

Pansy was afraid to walk into
e garden because her friends
told her there were hawks
foxes and dragons hiding there
ut Violet smiled and explained
they are hollyhocks and
xgloves, and snapdragons
and that everyone knows
owers would never hurt you —
not even the tigerlillies!

Bottom Right

We are just as different as we can be, But dearest friends we will always be.

All Bears are photographed on pages 56–57.

Sample Information

The Parasol Bear sample was stitched on carnation pink Jubilee 28 over two threads. The finished design size is 5¾" x 6¾". The fabric was cut 12" x 13". Graph is on page 67.

Stitch Count: 81 x 95

Other Fabrics	Finished Size
Aida 11	7⅜" x 8⅝"
Aida 18	4½" x 5¼"
Hardanger 22	3⅝" x 4⅜"

Anchor		DMC	

Step 1: Cross Stitch (2 strands)

Anchor		DMC	
926	–		Ecru
301		744	Yellow–pale
890		729	Old Gold–med.
25		3326	Rose–lt.
69		3687	Mauve
117	○	3747	Blue Violet–vy. lt.
154		3755	Baby Blue
921		931	Antique Blue–med.
203		954	Nile Green
210		562	Jade–med.
878	M	501	Blue Green–dk.
801	△	501	Blue Green–dk. (1 strand)
150		823	Navy Blue–dk. (1 strand)
362		437	Tan–lt.
362		437	Tan–lt. (1 strand)
338		3776	Mahogany–lt. (1 strand)
349		301	Mahogany–med.
349	E	301	Mahogany–med. (1 strand)
357		801	Coffee Brown–dk. (1 strand)
379		840	Beige Brown–med.
380		839	Beige Brown–dk.
382	×	3371	Black Brown

Step 2: Backstitch (1 strand)

Anchor		DMC	
926			Ecru (2 strands)
150		823	Navy Blue–dk.
357		801	Coffee Brown–dk.
382		3371	Black Brown

Step 3: Wrapped Backstitch

Anchor		DMC	
890		729	Old Gold–med.

Step 4: French Knot (1 strand)

Anchor		DMC	
926			Ecru

Sample Information

The Quilting Bear sample was stitched on ivory Annabelle 28 over two threads. The finished design size is 4⅞" x 7⅜". The fabric was cut 11" x 14". Graph is on page 68.

Stitch Count: 69 x 103

Other Fabrics	Finished Size
Aida 11	6¼" x 9⅜"
Aida 18	3⅞" x 5¾"
Hardanger 22	3⅛" x 4⅝"

Step 1: Cross Stitch (2 strands)

Anchor		DMC	
926	–		Ecru
300	·	745	Yellow–lt. pale
891	×	676	Old Gold–lt.
11		351	Coral
13		350	Coral–med.
19		817	Coral Red–vy. dk.
20	N	498	Christmas Red–dk.
117	○	3747	Blue Violet–vy. lt.
160		3761	Sky Blue–lt.
161		3760	Wedgwood–med.
779	✳	926	Slate Green
362		437	Tan–lt.
362		437	Tan–lt. (1 strand)
338		3776	Mahogany–lt. (1 strand)
349	E	301	Mahogany–med.
349		301	Mahogany–med. (1 strand)
357		801	Coffee Brown–dk. (1 strand)
379		840	Beige Brown–med.
380		839	Beige Brown–dk.
382	△	3371	Black Brown

Step 2: Backstitch (1 strand)

Anchor		DMC	
926			Ecru (2 strands)
20		498	Christmas Red–dk.
161		3760	Wedgwood–med.
382		3371	Black Brown

Step 3: French Knot (1 strand)

Anchor		DMC	
926	○		Ecru
891	●	676	Old Gold–lt.

Step 4: Lazy Daisy Stitch (1 strand)

Anchor		DMC	
161		3760	Wedgwood–med.

Parasol Bear

Sample Information

The Bear & Bunny sample was stitched on pewter Murano 30 over two threads. The finished design size is 4⅜" x 6¾". The fabric was cut 11" x 13". Graph is on page 70.

Stitch Count: 66 x 102

Other Fabrics	Finished Size
Aida 11	6" x 9¼"
Aida 14	4¾" x 7¼"
Aida 18	3⅝" x 5⅝"
Hardanger 22	3" x 4⅝"

Anchor   DMC

Step 1: Cross Stitch (2 strands)

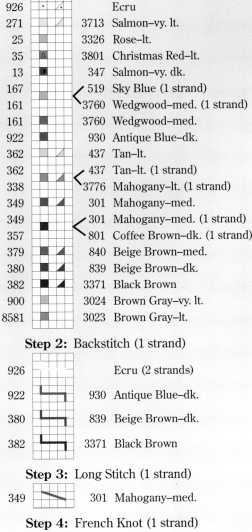

Anchor	DMC	
926		Ecru
271	3713	Salmon–vy. lt.
25	3326	Rose–lt.
35	3801	Christmas Red–lt.
13	347	Salmon–vy. dk.
167	519	Sky Blue (1 strand)
161	3760	Wedgwood–med. (1 strand)
161	3760	Wedgwood–med.
922	930	Antique Blue–dk.
362	437	Tan–lt.
362	437	Tan–lt. (1 strand)
338	3776	Mahogany–lt. (1 strand)
349	301	Mahogany–med.
349	301	Mahogany–med. (1 strand)
357	801	Coffee Brown–dk. (1 strand)
379	840	Beige Brown–med.
380	839	Beige Brown–dk.
382	3371	Black Brown
900	3024	Brown Gray–vy. lt.
8581	3023	Brown Gray–lt.

Step 2: Backstitch (1 strand)

926		Ecru (2 strands)
922	930	Antique Blue–dk.
380	839	Beige Brown–dk.
382	3371	Black Brown

Step 3: Long Stitch (1 strand)

349	301	Mahogany–med.

Step 4: French Knot (1 strand)

926		Ecru

Sample Information

The Bear & Sandcastle sample was stitched on summer khaki Cashel linen 28 over two threads. The finished design size is 6¼" x 6⅛". The fabric was cut 13" x 13". Graph is on page 71.

Stitch Count: 87 x 86

Other Fabrics	Finished Size
Aida 11	7⅞" x 7⅞"
Aida 18	4⅞" x 4¾"
Hardanger 22	4" x 3⅞"

Anchor   DMC

Step 1: Cross Stitch (2 strands)

Anchor	DMC	
300	745	Yellow–lt. pale
891	676	Old Gold–lt.
25	3326	Rose–lt.
27	899	Rose–med. (1 strand)
42	335	Rose (1 strand)
42	335	Rose (1 strand)
871	3041	Antique Violet–med. (1 strand)
35	3801	Christmas Red–lt.
13	349	Coral–dk.
160	813	Blue–lt.
921	931	Antique Blue–med.
942	738	Tan–vy. lt.
942	738	Tan–vy. lt. (1 strand)
363	436	Tan (1 strand)
363	436	Tan (1 strand)
970	3726	Antique Mauve–dk. (1 strand)
362	437	Tan–lt.
362	437	Tan–lt. (1 strand)
338	3776	Mahogany–lt. (1 strand)
349	301	Mahogany–med.
349	301	Mahogany–med. (1 strand)
357	801	Coffee Brown–dk. (1 strand)
379	840	Beige Brown–med.
380	839	Beige Brown–dk.
382	3371	Black Brown

Step 2: Backstitch (1 strand)

926		Ecru (2 strands)
970	3726	Antique Mauve–dk.
357	801	Coffee Brown–dk.
382	3371	Black Brown

Step 3: French Knot (1 strand)

926		Ecru

Bear & Sandcastle

Additional Verse

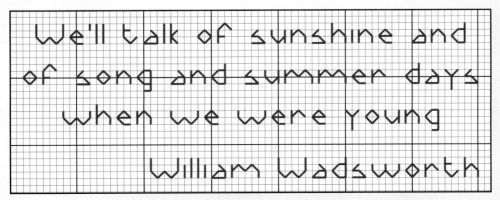

We'll talk of sunshine and
of song and summer days
when we were young

William Wadsworth

Sample Information

The Fishing Bear sample was stitched on amaretto Jubilee 28 over two threads. The finished design size is 4⅞" x 6⅝". The fabric was cut 11" x 13". Graph is on opposite page.

Stitch Count: 68 x 93

Other Fabrics	Finished Size
Aida 11	6⅛" x 8½"
Aida 18	3¾" x 5⅛"
Hardanger 22	3⅛" x 4¼"

Anchor   DMC

Step 1: Cross Stitch (2 strands)

Anchor	DMC	
926		Ecru
891	676	Old Gold–lt.
13	347	Salmon–vy. dk.
872	3740	Antique Violet–dk.
160	3761	Sky Blue–lt.
154	3755	Baby Blue
921	931	Antique Blue–med.
217	3815	Celadon Green–dk.
851	924	Slate Green–vy. dk.
362	437	Tan–lt.
362	437	Tan–lt. (1 strand)
338	3776	Mahogany–lt. (1 strand)
349	301	Mahogany–med.
349	301	Mahogany–med. (1 strand)
357	801	Coffee Brown–dk. (1 strand)
379	840	Beige Brown–med.
380	839	Beige Brown–dk.
382	3371	Black Brown
1048	921	Copper
341	919	Red Copper
352	300	Mahogany–vy. dk.
942	738	Tan–vy. lt.
363	436	Tan

Step 2: Backstitch (1 strand)

Anchor	DMC	
926		Ecru (2 strands)
13	347	Salmon–vy. dk.
872	3740	Antique Violet–dk.
851	924	Slate Green–vy. dk.
382	3371	Black Brown

Step 3: Long Stitch (1 strand)

Anchor	DMC	
154	3755	Baby Blue
349	301	Mahogany–med. (2 strands)

Anchor	DMC	
926		Ecru
872	3740	Antique Violet–vy. dk.
380	839	Beige Brown–dk.

Sample Information

The Sailor Bear sample was stitched on periwinkle Pastel linen 28 over two threads. The finished design size is 5⅛" x 6¼". The fabric was cut 12" x 13". Graph is on page 74.

Stitch Count: 71 x 87

Other Fabrics	Finished Size
Aida 11	6½" x 7⅞"
Aida 18	4" x 4⅞"
Hardanger 22	3¼" x 4"

Anchor   DMC

Step 1: Cross Stitch (2 strands)

Anchor	DMC	
1		White
926		Ecru
300	3823	Yellow–ultra pale
891	676	Old Gold–lt.
11	3328	Salmon–dk.
13	347	Salmon–vy. dk.
117	341	Blue Violet–lt.
154	3755	Baby Blue
978	322	Navy Blue–vy. lt.
147	312	Navy Blue–lt.
149	336	Navy Blue
362	437	Tan–lt.
362	437	Tan–lt. (1 strand)
338	3776	Mahogany–lt. (1 strand)
349	301	Mahogany–med.
349	301	Mahogany–med. (1 strand)
357	801	Coffee Brown–dk. (1 strand)
379	840	Beige Brown–med.
380	839	Beige Brown–dk.
382	3371	Black Brown
8581	646	Beaver Gray–dk.
401	844	Beaver Gray–ultra dk.

Step 2: Backstitch (1 strand)

Anchor	DMC	
926		Ecru (2 strands)
149	336	Navy Blue
349	301	Mahogany–med.
382	3371	Black Brown
8581	646	Beaver Gray–dk.
401	844	Beaver Gray–ultra dk.

Step 3: French Knot (1 strand)

Anchor	DMC	
926		Ecru

Fishing Bear

Sailor Bear

Sample Information

The Noah's Ark Bear sample was stitched on dirty linen Cashel 28 over two threads. The finished design size is 4⅝" x 5⅝". The fabric was cut 11" x 12". Graph is on page 76.

Stitch Count: 65 x 79

Other Fabrics	Finished Size
Aida 11	5⅞" x 7⅛"
Aida 18	3⅝" x 4⅜"
Hardanger 22	3" x 3⅝"

Anchor   **DMC**

Step 1: Cross Stitch (2 strands)

Anchor		DMC	
926			Ecru
297		743	Yellow–med.
886		677	Old Gold–vy. lt.
891		676	Old Gold–lt.
373		3045	Yellow Beige–dk.
159		3325	Baby Blue–lt.
145		334	Baby Blue–med.
145		334	Baby Blue–med. (1 strand)
922		930	Antique Blue–dk. (1 strand)
308		976	Golden Brown–med.
339		920	Copper–med.
362		437	Tan–lt.
362		437	Tan–lt. (1 strand)
338		3776	Mahogany–lt. (1 strand)
338		3776	Mahogany–lt.
349		301	Mahogany–med.
349		301	Mahogany–med. (1 strand)
357		801	Coffee Brown–dk. (1 strand)
379		840	Beige Brown–med.
380		839	Beige Brown–dk.
382		3371	Black Brown
900		3024	Brown Gray–vy. lt.
8581		647	Beaver Gray–med.
905		646	Beaver Gray–dk.
403		310	Black

Step 2: Backstitch (1 strand)

Anchor	DMC	
926		Ecru (2 strands)
922	930	Antique Blue–dk.
382	3371	Black Brown
403	310	Black

Step 3: French Knot (1 strand)

Anchor	DMC	
926		Ecru
382	3371	Black Brown

Sample Information

The Santa Bear sample was stitched on silver-white Lugana 25 over two threads. The finished design size is 6⅛" x 7¼". The fabric was cut 13" x 14". Graph is on page 77.

Stitch Count: 76 x 90

Other Fabrics	Finished Size
Aida 11	6⅞" x 8⅛"
Aida 14	5½" x 6⅜"
Aida 18	4¼" x 5"
Hardanger 22	3½" x 4⅛"

Anchor   **DMC**

Step 1: Cross Stitch (2 strands)

Anchor		DMC	
926			Ecru
886		677	Old Gold–vy. lt.
891		676	Old Gold–lt.
891		3045	Yellow Beige–dk.
907		3821	Straw
10		3712	Salmon–med.
13		347	Salmon–vy. dk.
20		498	Christmas Red–dk.
72		902	Garnet–vy. dk.
921		931	Antique Blue–med.
149		311	Navy Blue–med.
150		823	Navy Blue–dk.
265		3348	Yellow Green–lt.
216		367	Pistachio Green–dk.
363		437	Tan–lt.
363		437	Tan–lt. (1 strand)
338		3776	Mahogany–lt. (1 strand)
349		301	Mahogany–med.
349		301	Mahogany–med. (1 strand)
357		801	Coffee Brown–dk. (1 strand)
379		840	Beige Brown–med.
380		839	Beige Brown–dk.
382		3371	Black Brown
900		3023	Brown Gray–lt.
8581		646	Beaver Gray–dk.
399		318	Steel Gray–lt.

Step 2: Backstitch (1 strand)

Anchor	DMC	
926		Ecru (2 strands)
72	902	Garnet–vy. dk.
150	823	Navy Blue–dk.
357	801	Coffee Brown–dk.
382	3371	Black Brown

Step 3: Long Stitch (2 strands)

Anchor	DMC	
349	301	Mahogany–med.

Step 4: French Knot (1 strand)

Anchor	DMC	
926		Ecru

Noah's Ark Bear

Additional Verse

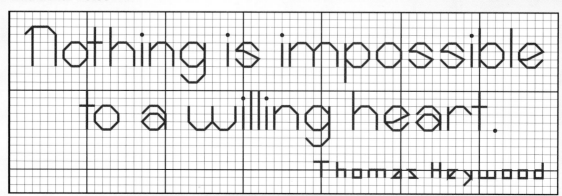

Santa Bear

Sample Information

The Angel Bear sample was stitched on wood violet linen 28 over two threads. The finished design size is 6⅜" x 5⅞". The fabric was cut 13" x 12".

Stitch Count: 92 x 82

Other Fabrics	Finished Size
Aida 11	8⅜" x 7½"
Aida 18	5⅛" x 4½"
Hardanger 22	4⅛" x 3¾"

Anchor	DMC

Step 1: Cross Stitch (2 strands)

926		Ecru
297		743	Yellow–med.

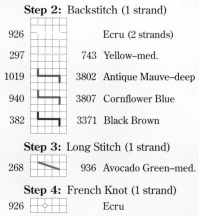

307	783	Christmas Gold
25	3326	Rose–lt.
11	351	Coral
27	899	Rose–med. (1 strand)
42	335	Rose (1 strand)
42	335	Rose (1 strand)
1019	3802	Antique Mauve–deep (1 strand)
1019	3802	Antique Mauve–deep
117	3747	Blue Violet–vy. lt.
870	3042	Antique Violet–lt.
268	936	Avocado Green–med.
362	437	Tan–lt.
362	437	Tan–lt. (1 strand)
338	3776	Mahogany–lt. (1 strand)
349	301	Mahogany–med.
349	301	Mahogany–med. (1 strand)
357	801	Coffee Brown–dk. (1 strand)
379	840	Beige Brown–med.
380	839	Beige Brown–dk.
382	3371	Black Brown

Step 2: Backstitch (1 strand)

926		Ecru (2 strands)
297		743	Yellow–med.
1019		3802	Antique Mauve–deep
940		3807	Cornflower Blue
382		3371	Black Brown

Step 3: Long Stitch (1 strand)

268		936	Avocado Green–med.

Step 4: French Knot (1 strand)

926		Ecru

Angel Bear

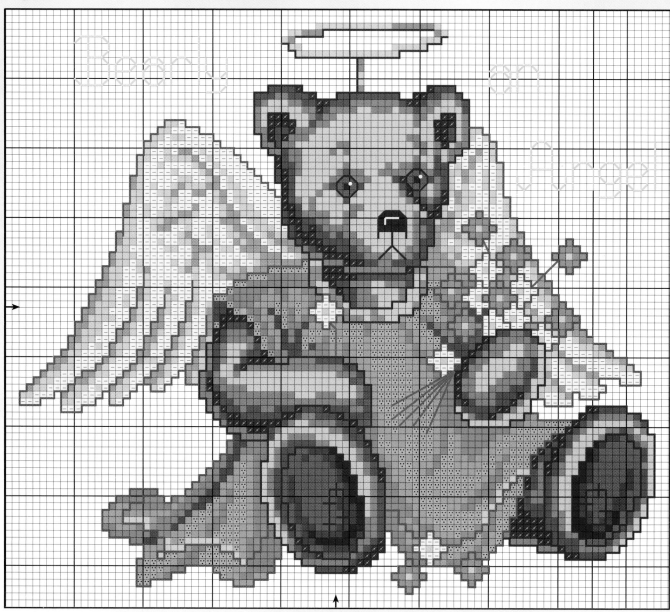

"Don't part with your illusions. When they are gone... you have ceased to live."
—Mark Twain

Photograph on page 58. Code and sample information on page 81.

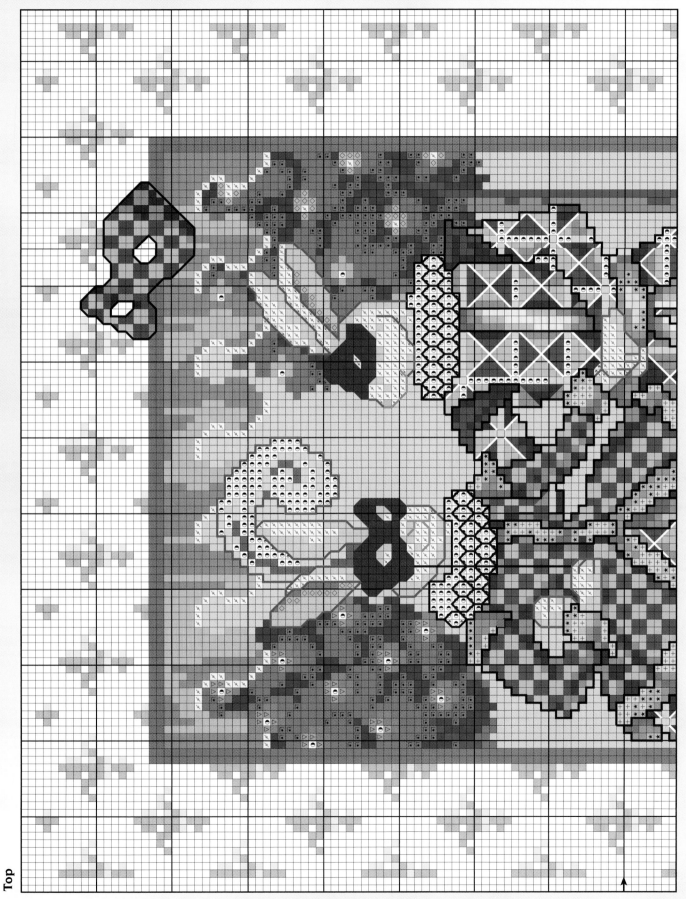

Top

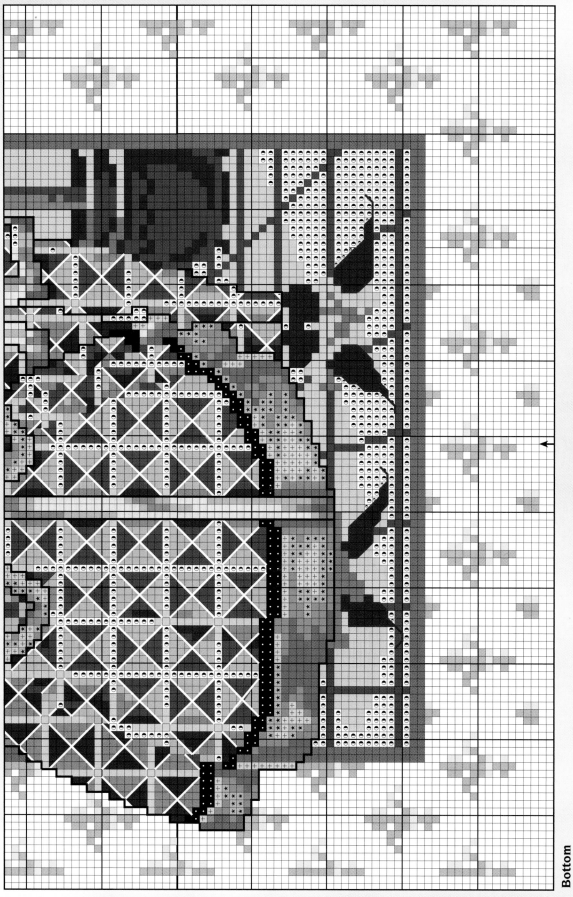

Bottom

Sample Information

The sample was stitched on black Dublin linen 25 over two threads. The finished design size is 9⅛" x 12½". The fabric was cut 16" x 19".

Stitch Count: 114 x 156

Other Fabrics	Finished Size
Aida 11	10⅜" x 14⅛"
Aida 14	8⅛" x 11⅛"
Aida 18	6⅜" x 8⅝"
Hardanger 22	5⅛" x 7⅛"

Anchor		DMC	

Step 1: Cross Stitch (2 strands)

Anchor		DMC	
1			White
926			Ecru
301		744	Yellow–pale
886		677	Old Gold–vy. lt.
891		676	Old Gold–lt.
907		3821	Straw
307		783	Christmas Gold
373		3045	Yellow Beige–dk.
323		722	Orange Spice–lt.
8		761	Salmon–lt.
9		760	Salmon
11		3328	Salmon–dk.
896		3722	Shell Pink
160		3761	Sky Blue–lt.
145		334	Baby Blue–med.
147		312	Navy Blue–lt.
150		823	Navy Blue–dk.
859		3052	Green Gray–med.
846		3051	Green Gray–dk.
879		500	Blue Green–vy. dk.
376		842	Beige Brown–vy. lt.
379		840	Beige Brown–med.
942		738	Tan–vy. lt.
370		434	Brown–lt.
936		632	Pecan–dk.
403		310	Black

Step 2: Backstitch (1 strand)

Anchor		DMC	
11		3328	Salmon–dk. (2 strands)
379		840	Beige Brown–med.
936		632	Pecan–dk.
403		310	Black

Step 3: Long Stitch (2 strands)

Anchor		DMC	
1			White
150		823	Navy Blue–dk.

"He that is of a merry heart, hath a continual feast."
—Proverbs 15:15

Photograph on page 59.

Sample Information

The sample was stitched on black Dublin linen 25 over two threads. The finished design size is 9" x 12½". The fabric was cut 15" x 19". Graph begins on page 82.

Anchor		DMC	

Step 1: Cross Stitch (2 strands)

Anchor		DMC	
1			White
926			Ecru
886		677	Old Gold–vy. lt.
891		676	Old Gold–lt.
907		3821	Straw
307		783	Christmas Gold
373		3045	Yellow Beige–dk.
907		3825	Straw
323		722	Orange Spice–lt. (1 strand)
324		721	Orange Spice–med. (1 strand)
324		721	Orange Spice–med. (1 strand)
896		3721	Shell Pink–dk. (1 strand)
49		963	Wild Rose–vy. lt.
25		3326	Rose–lt. (1 strand)
10		3712	Salmon–med. (1 strand)
10		3712	Salmon–med.
11		3328	Salmon–dk.
13		347	Salmon–vy. dk.
897		221	Shell Pink–vy. dk.
95		554	Violet–lt.
105		208	Lavender–vy. dk.
871		3041	Antique Violet–med.
159		827	Blue–vy. lt.
130		799	Delft–med.
978		322	Navy Blue–lt.
816		3750	Antique Blue–vy. dk.
265		3348	Yellow Green–lt.
266		3347	Yellow Green–med.
266		3347	Yellow Green–med. (1 strand)
862		520	Fern Green–dk. (1 strand)
862		520	Fern Green–dk.
842		3013	Khaki Green–lt.
861		3363	Pine Green–med.
879		500	Blue Green–vy. dk.
885		738	Tan–ultra vy. lt.
899		3782	Mocha Brown–lt.
379		840	Beige Brown–med.
380		839	Beige Brown–dk.
403		310	Black

Stitch Count: 113 x 156

Other Fabrics	Finished Size
Aida 11	10¼" x 14⅛"
Aida 14	8⅛" x 11⅛"
Aida 18	6¼" x 8⅝"
Hardanger 22	5⅛" x 7⅛"

Step 2: Backstitch (1 strand)

Anchor		DMC	
11		3328	Salmon–dk.
266		3347	Yellow Green–med. (2 strands)
842		3013	Khaki Green–lt.
380		839	Beige Brown–dk.
403		310	Black

Step 3: Long Stitch (1 strand)

Anchor		DMC	
403		310	Black (wand in

Step 4: French Knot (1 strand)

Anchor		DMC	
266		3347	Yellow Green–med.

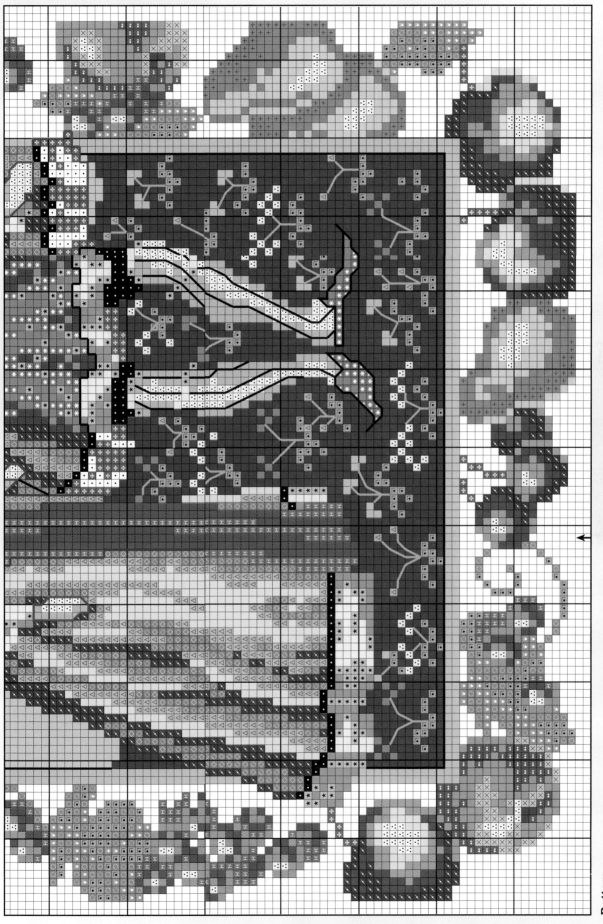

"Nothing can be truer than fairy wisdom. It is as true as sunbeams."

—Douglas Terrold

Photograph on page 60.

Sample Information

The sample was stitched on mint Jubilee 28 over two threads. The finished design size is 8⅞" x 10¾". The fabric was cut 15" x 17".

Stitch Count: 125 x 151

Other Fabrics	Finished Size
Aida 11	11⅜" x 13¾"
Aida 18	7" x 8⅜"
Hardanger 22	5⅝" x 6⅞"

Anchor   DMC

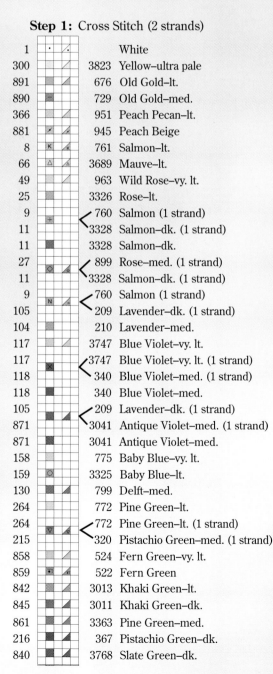

Step 1: Cross Stitch (2 strands)

Anchor	DMC	Color
1		White
300	3823	Yellow–ultra pale
891	676	Old Gold–lt.
890	729	Old Gold–med.
366	951	Peach Pecan–lt.
881	945	Peach Beige
8	761	Salmon–lt.
66	3689	Mauve–lt.
49	963	Wild Rose–vy. lt.
25	3326	Rose–lt.
9	760	Salmon (1 strand)
11	3328	Salmon–dk. (1 strand)
11	3328	Salmon–dk.
27	899	Rose–med. (1 strand)
11	3328	Salmon–dk. (1 strand)
9	760	Salmon (1 strand)
105	209	Lavender–dk. (1 strand)
104	210	Lavender–med.
117	3747	Blue Violet–vy. lt.
117	3747	Blue Violet–vy. lt. (1 strand)
118	340	Blue Violet–med. (1 strand)
118	340	Blue Violet–med.
105	209	Lavender–dk. (1 strand)
871	3041	Antique Violet–med. (1 strand)
871	3041	Antique Violet–med.
158	775	Baby Blue–vy. lt.
159	3325	Baby Blue–lt.
130	799	Delft–med.
264	772	Pine Green–lt.
264	772	Pine Green–lt. (1 strand)
215	320	Pistachio Green–med. (1 strand)
858	524	Fern Green–vy. lt.
859	522	Fern Green
842	3013	Khaki Green–lt.
845	3011	Khaki Green–dk.
861	3363	Pine Green–med.
216	367	Pistachio Green–dk.
840	3768	Slate Green–dk.

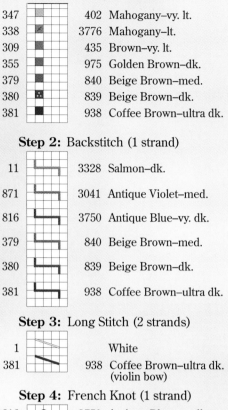

Anchor	DMC	Color
347	402	Mahogany–vy. lt.
338	3776	Mahogany–lt.
309	435	Brown–vy. lt.
355	975	Golden Brown–dk.
379	840	Beige Brown–med.
380	839	Beige Brown–dk.
381	938	Coffee Brown–ultra dk.

Step 2: Backstitch (1 strand)

Anchor	DMC	Color
11	3328	Salmon–dk.
871	3041	Antique Violet–med.
816	3750	Antique Blue–vy. dk.
379	840	Beige Brown–med.
380	839	Beige Brown–dk.
381	938	Coffee Brown–ultra dk.

Step 3: Long Stitch (2 strands)

Anchor	DMC	Color
1		White
381	938	Coffee Brown–ultra dk. (violin bow)

Step 4: French Knot (1 strand)

Anchor	DMC	Color
816	3750	Antique Blue–vy. dk.

Additional Verse

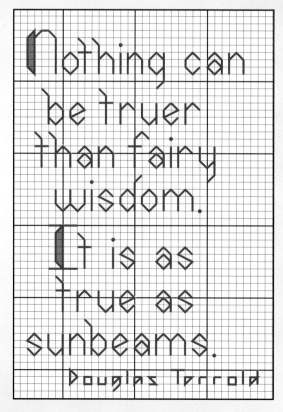

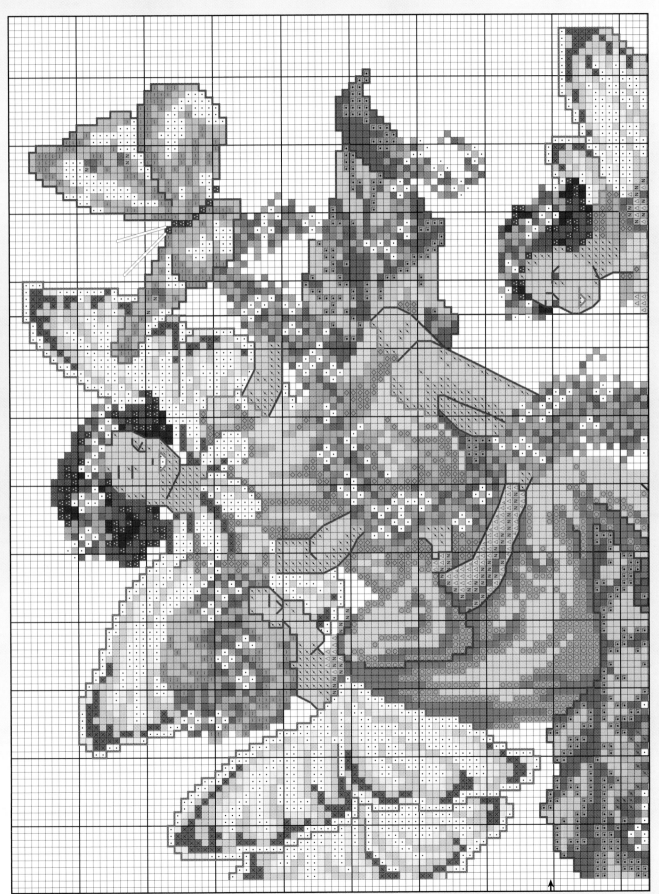

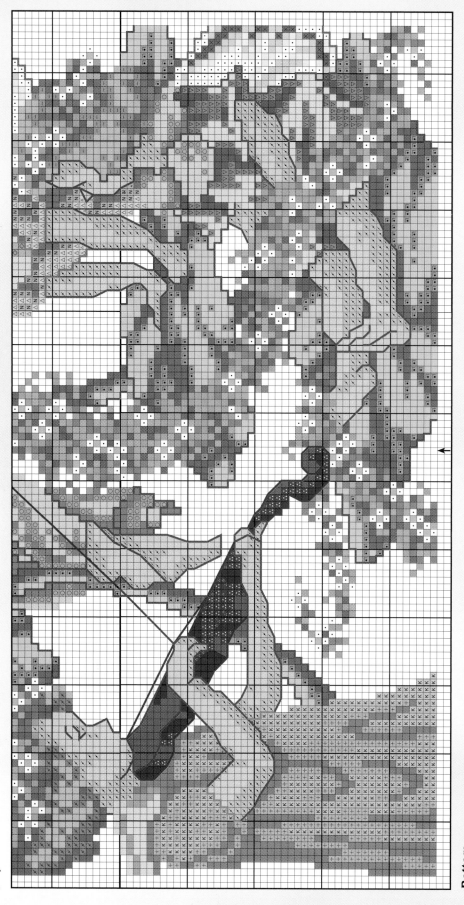

We have loved the stars too fondly to be fearful of the night.

Photograph on page 61.

Anchor   DMC

Step 1: Cross Stitch (2 strands)

386		746	Off White
300		745	Yellow–lt.
891		676	Old Gold–lt.
366		951	Peach Pecan–lt.
881		945	Peach Beige
868		758	Terra Cotta–lt.
337		3778	Terra Cotta
892		225	Shell Pink–vy. lt.
893		224	Shell Pink–lt.
894		223	Shell Pink–med.
896		3721	Shell Pink–dk.
1019		3802	Antique Mauve–deep
8		761	Salmon–lt.
10		3712	Salmon–med.
13		347	Salmon–vy. dk.
47		304	Christmas Red–med.
43		815	Garnet–med.
875		503	Blue Green–med.
876		502	Blue Green
878		501	Blue Green–dk.
879		500	Blue Green–vy. dk.
888		3828	Hazel Nut Brown
373		420	Hazel Nut Brown–dk.
347		402	Mahogany–vy. lt.
338		3776	Mahogany–lt.
355		975	Golden Brown–dk.
357		801	Coffee Brown–dk.

Step 2: Backstitch (1 strand)

386		746	Off White (1 strand)
		032	Gold Cord (2 strands)
896		3721	Shell Pink–dk.
43		815	Garnet–med.
879		500	Blue Green–vy. dk.
944		869	Hazel Nut Brown–vy. dk.
357		801	Coffee Brown–dk.

Step 3: Long Stitch (2 strands)

| | | 002C | Gold Cord |

Step 4: French Knot (1 strand)

| 896 | | 3721 | Shell Pink–dk. |

Step 5: Eyelet Stitch (2 strands)

| 891 | | 676 | Old Gold–lt. |

Sample Information

The sample was stitched on steel gray Belfast linen 32 over two threads. The finished design size is 11⅜" x 12⅛". The fabric was cut 18" x 19". Graph begins on page 88.

Stitch Count: 159 x 169

Other Fabrics	Finished Size
Aida 11	14½" x 15⅜"
Aida 14	11⅜" x 12⅛"
Aida 18	8⅞" x 9⅜"
Hardanger 22	7¼" x 7⅝"

Additional Verse

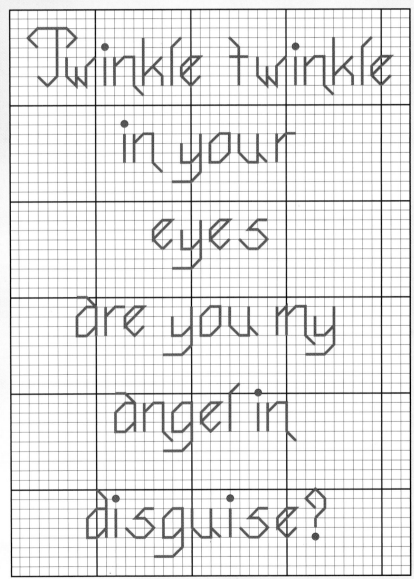

Life is filled with
as many possibilities
as there are stars
in the sky.

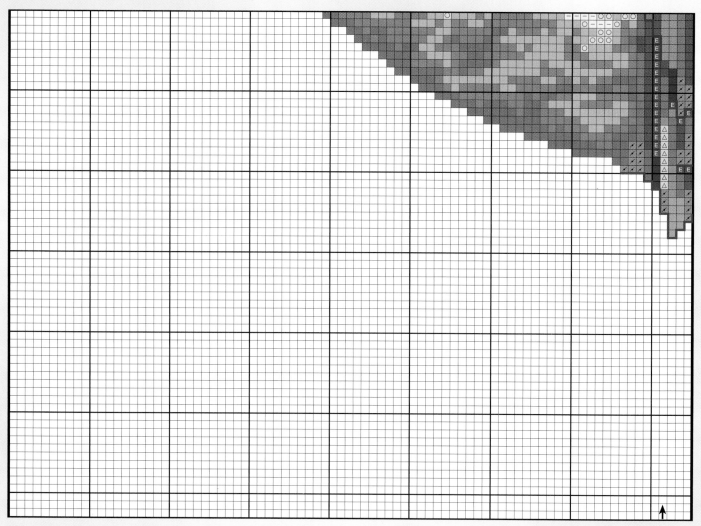

Bottom Left

Additional Verse

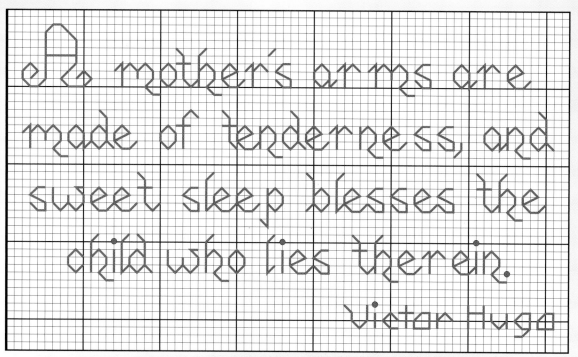

A mother's arms are made of tenderness, and sweet sleep blesses the child who lies therein.

Victor Hugo

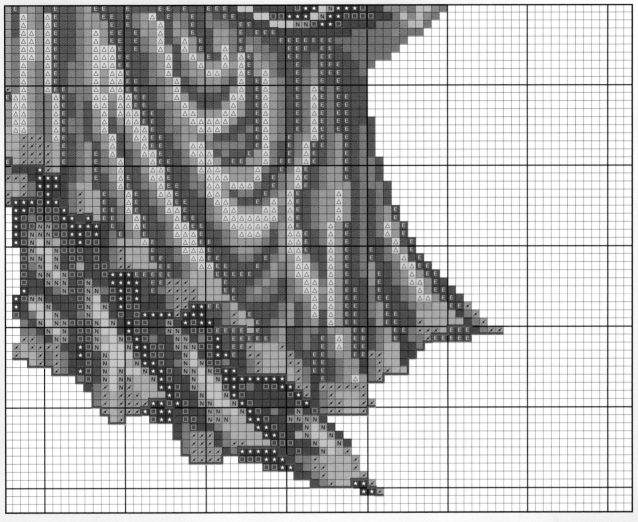

Bottom Right

Additional Verse

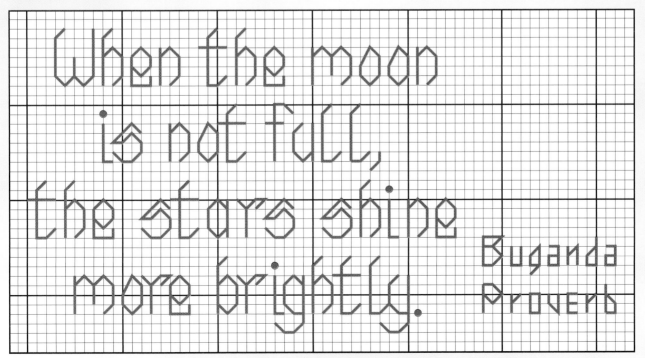

When the moon
is not full,
the stars shine
more brightly.

Buganda
Proverb

All creatures great and small

All things bright and beautiful

All things wise and wonderful

The Lord God made them All.

Photograph on page 92.

Additional Verse

Sample Information

The sample was stitched on navy Lugana 25 over two threads. The finished design size is 6¾" x 8¾". The fabric was cut 13" x 15".

Stitch Count: 85 x 109

Other Fabrics	Finished Size
Aida 11	7¾" x 9⅞"
Aida 14	6⅛" x 7¾"
Aida 18	4¾" x 6"
Hardanger 22	3⅞" x 5"

Anchor   DMC

Step 1: Cross Stitch (2 strands)

Anchor		DMC	
1			White
297		743	Yellow–med.
307		783	Christmas Gold
881		945	Peach Beige
11		351	Coral
13		347	Salmon–vy. dk.
43		815	Garnet–med.
843		3364	Pine Green
843		3364	Pine Green (1 strand)
846		3051	Green Gray–dk. (1 strand)
862		935	Avocado Green–dk.
347		402	Mahogany–vy. lt. (1 strand)
338		3776	Mahogany–lt. (1 strand)
349		921	Copper
351		400	Mahogany–dk.
1			White (1 strand)
830		644	Beaver Gray–med. (1 strand)
830		644	Beaver Gray–med.
392		642	Beige Gray–dk.
903		640	Beige Gray–vy. dk.
905		3781	Mocha Brown–dk.

Step 2: Backstitch (1 strand)

Anchor		DMC	
1			White (2 strands)
297		743	Yellow–med. (2 strands)
43		815	Garnet–med.
905		3781	Mocha Brown–dk.

Step 3: French Knot (1 strand)

Anchor		DMC	
297		743	Yellow–med.
13		347	Salmon–vy. dk.

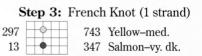

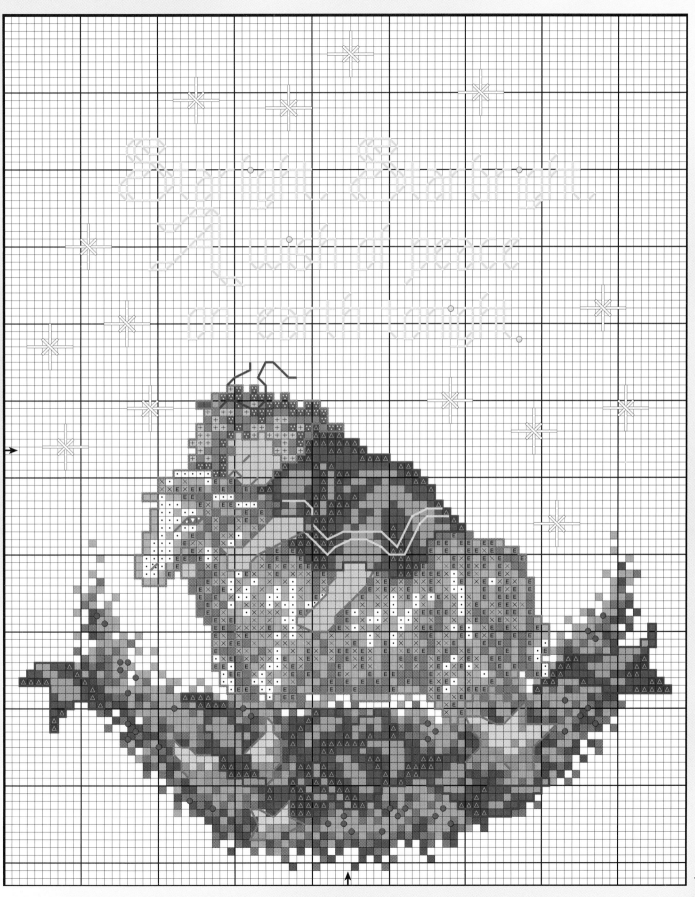

Mary & Jesus

Unto us a child is born. Unto us a child is given.

Photograph on page 93.

Sample Information

The sample was stitched on lt. mocha Cashel linen 28 over two threads. The finished design size is 5¾" x 14¼". The fabric was cut 12" x 21".

Stitch Count: 80 x 200

Other Fabrics	Finished Size
Aida 11	7¼" x 18⅛"
Aida 18	4½" x 11⅛"
Hardanger 22	3⅝" x 9⅛"

Anchor   **DMC**

Step 1: Cross Stitch (2 strands)

Anchor	DMC	
1		White
300	3823	Yellow–ultra pale
305	3822	Straw–lt.
907	3821	Straw
306	3820	Straw–dk.
891	676	Old Gold–lt.
308	782	Topaz–med.
366	951	Peach Pecan–lt.
881	945	Peach Beige
74	3354	Dusty Rose–vy. lt.
75	3733	Dusty Rose–lt. (1 strand)
69	3687	Mauve (1 strand)
69	3687	Mauve (1 strand)
78	3803	Mauve–dk. (1 strand)
104	210	Lavender–med.
110	208	Lavender–vy. dk.
101	327	Antique Violet–vy. dk.
117	340	Blue Violet–med.
118	3746	Blue Violet–dk.
119	333	Blue Violet–vy. dk. (1 strand)
99	550	Violet–vy. dk. (1 strand)
99	550	Violet–vy. dk. (1strand)
127	939	Navy Blue–vy. dk. (1 strand)
975	3753	Antique Blue–ultra vy. lt.
154	3755	Baby Blue
121	793	Cornflower Blue–med.
940	792	Cornflower Blue–dk.
941	791	Cornflower Blue–vy. dk.
127	939	Navy Blue–vy. dk.
858	524	Fern Green–vy. lt.
859	522	Fern Green
373	3045	Yellow Beige–dk.
888	3828	Hazel Nut Brown
830	644	Beige Gray–med.
392	642	Beige Gray–dk.
903	640	Beige Gray–vy. dk.
273	3787	Brown Gray–dk.
380	839	Beige Brown–dk.
381	938	Coffee Brown–ultra dk.

Step 2: Backstitch (1 strand)

Anchor	DMC	
306	3820	Straw–dk. (2 strands)
99	550	Violet–vy. dk.
127	939	Navy Blue–vy. dk.
859	522	Fern Green
273	3787	Brown Gray–dk.
380	839	Beige Brown–dk.
381	938	Coffee Brown–ultra dk. (eyebrows, eyelashes, mouths and Mary's hair)

Additional Verse

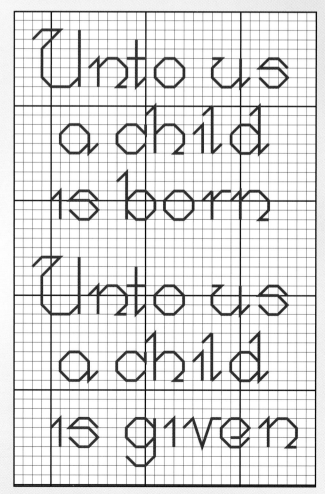

Bottom

"Faith, hope, and charity; but the greatest of these is charity."—1 Corinthians 13:13

Photograph on page 94.

Sample Information

The sample was stitched on platinum Belfast linen 32 over two threads. The finished design size is 14¼" x 22⅞". The fabric was cut 21" x 29". Graph begins on page 104.

Stitch Count: 228 x 366

Other Fabrics	Finished Size
Aida 11	20¾" x 33¼"
Aida 14	16¼" x 26⅛"
Aida 18	12⅝" x 20⅜"
Hardanger 22	10⅜" x 16⅝"

Anchor   DMC

Step 1: Cross Stitch (2 strands)

Anchor		DMC	
1			White
886		677	Old Gold–vy. lt.
891		676	Old Gold–lt.
366		951	Peach Pecan–lt.
868		758	Terra Cotta–lt.
8		353	Peach
11		350	Coral–med.
19		817	Coral Red–vy. dk.
43		815	Garnet–med.
128		800	Delft–pale
145		334	Baby Blue–med.
147		312	Navy Blue–lt.
150		823	Navy Blue–dk.
214		966	Baby Green–med.
215		320	Pistachio Green–med.
216		367	Pistachio Green–dk.
212		561	Jade–vy. dk.
879		500	Blue Green–vy. dk.
882		3773	Pecan–vy. lt.
914		3772	Pecan–med.
5975		356	Terra Cotta–med.
341		918	Red Copper–dk.
363		436	Tan
371		433	Brown–med.
380		839	Beige Brown–dk.
381		938	Coffee Brown–ultra dk.
900		3024	Brown Gray–vy. lt.
8581		3023	Brown Gray–lt.
397		762	Pearl Gray–vy. lt.
401		413	Pewter Gray–dk.
403		310	Black

Step 2: Backstitch (1 strand)

Anchor		DMC	
43		815	Garnet–med.
150		823	Navy Blue–dk.
879		500	Blue Green–vy. dk.
380		839	Beige Brown–dk.

Step 3: Long Stitch (1 strand)

Anchor		DMC	
1			White (2 strands)
380		839	Beige Brown–dk. (inside drum on Traditional Santa)

Step 4: Wrapped Backstitch

Anchor		DMC	
891		676	Old Gold–lt. (2 strands) (wrap with 002P Gold cable 1 strand)

Step 5: French Knots (1 strand)

Anchor		DMC	
891		676	Old Gold–lt.
380		839	Beige Brown–dk.

Step 6: Beads

	00479	White
	62032	Frosted Cranberry

Step 7: Diamond Eyelet Stitch (2 strands)

1		White

Additional Verse

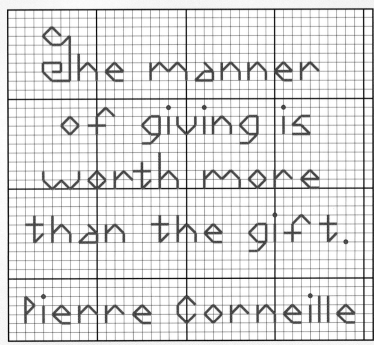

The manner of giving is worth more than the gift.

Pierre Corneille

Top Right

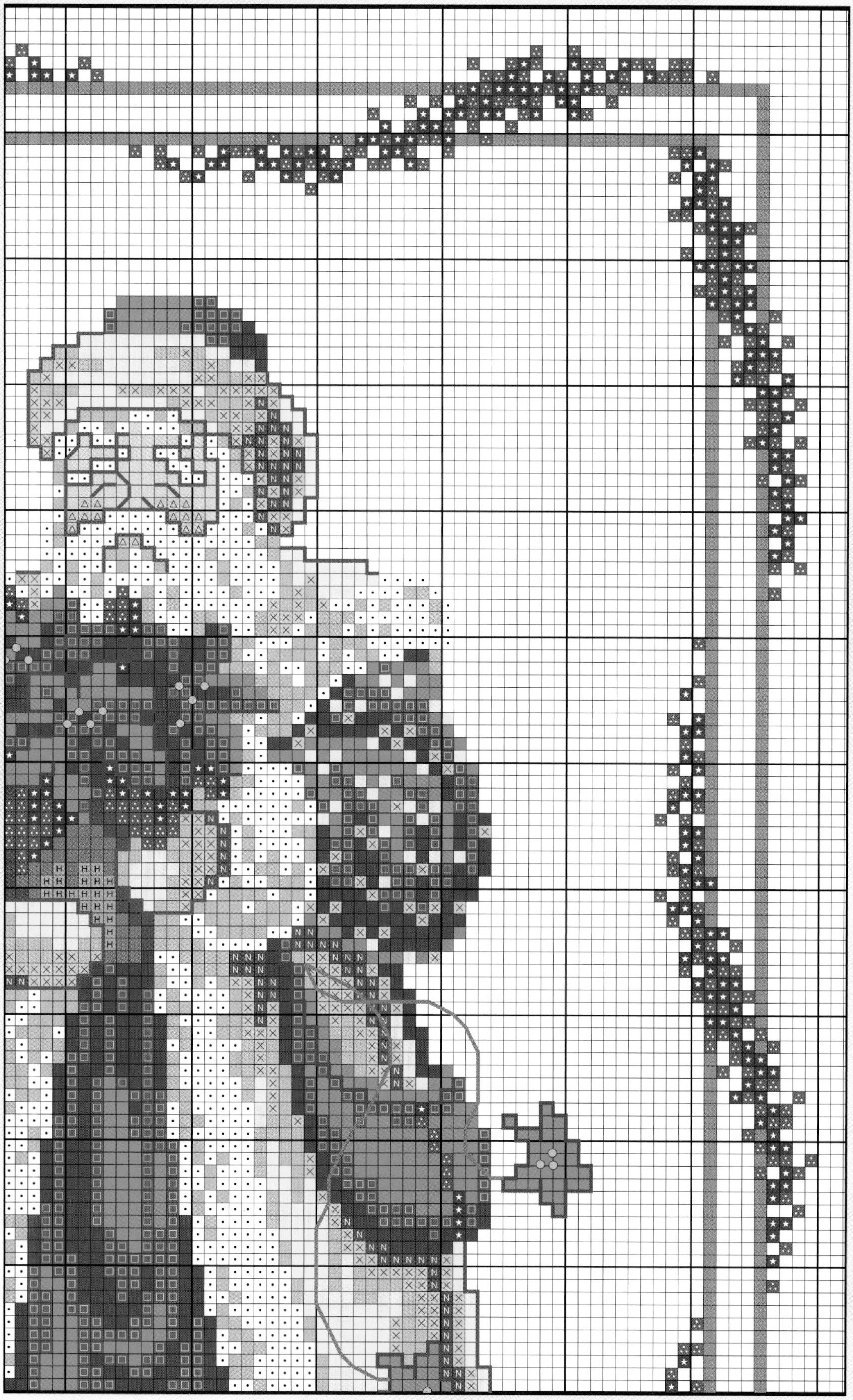

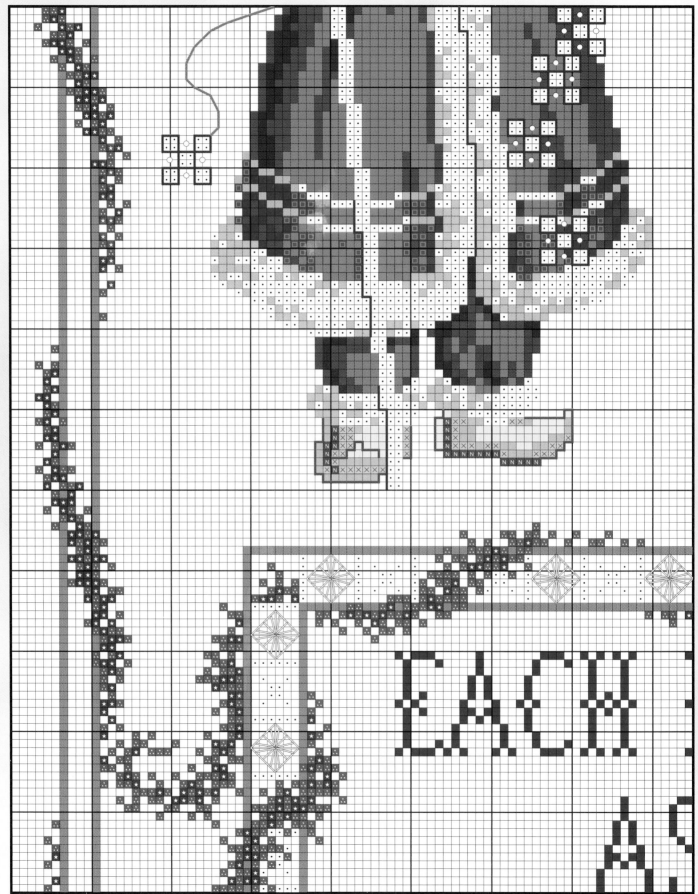

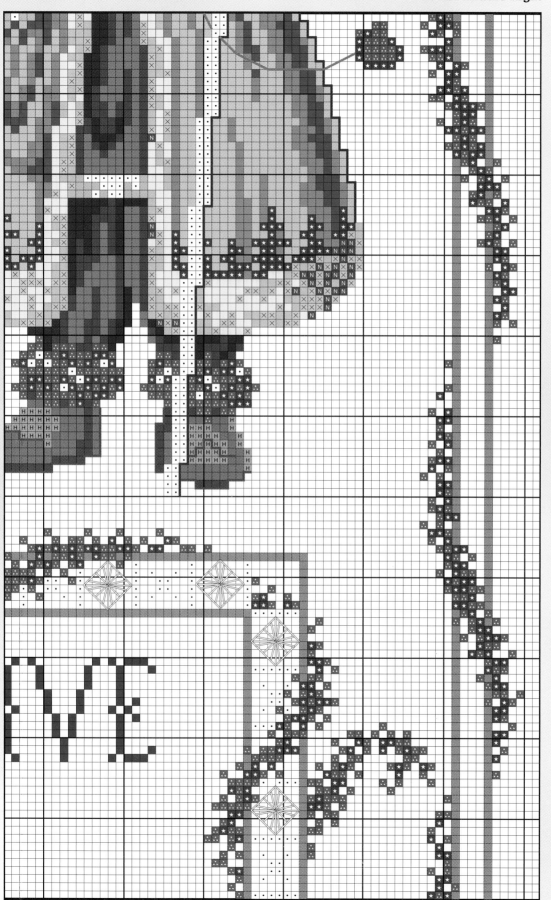

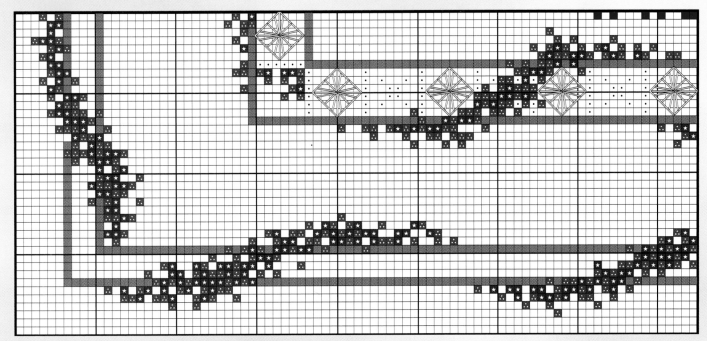

Bottom Left

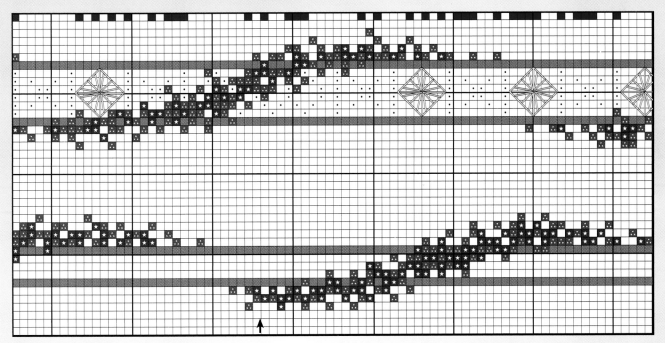

Bottom Center

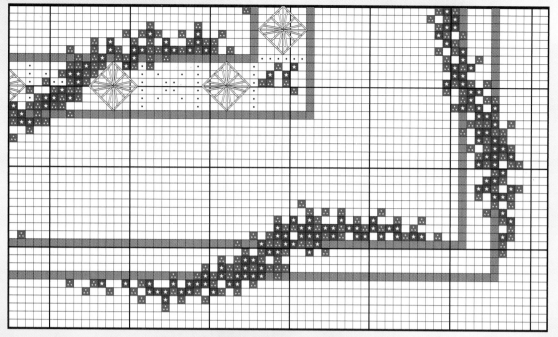

Bottom Right

Additional Verse

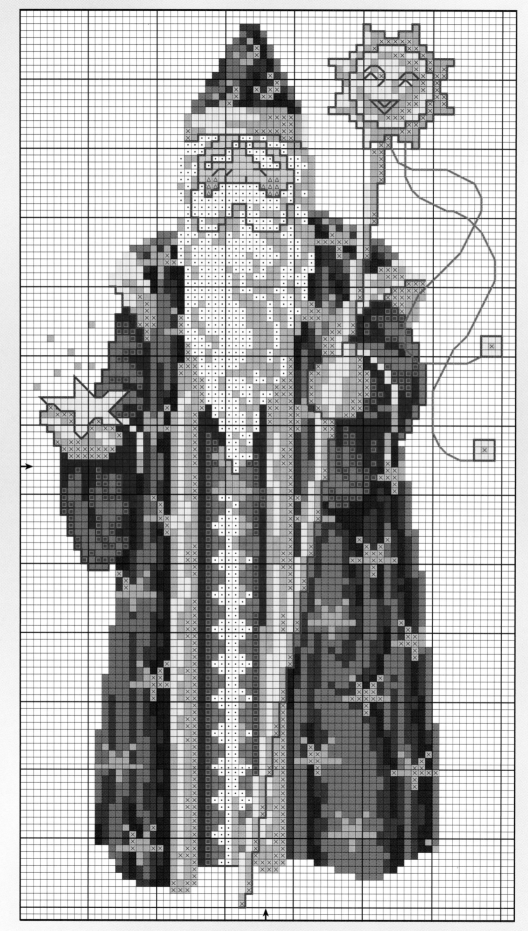

"The world is my country, all mankind are my brethren, and to do good is my religion."
—Thomas Paine

Photograph on page 95.

Sample Information

The sample was stitched on teal green Belfast linen 32 over two threads. The finished design size is 7¼" x 8½". The fabric was cut 14" x 15". Graph begins on page 118.

Stitch Count: 116 x 137

Other Fabrics	Finished Size
Aida 11	10½" x 12½"
Aida 14	8¼" x 9¾"
Aida 18	6½" x 7⅞"
Hardanger 22	5¼" x 6¼"

Anchor		DMC	

Step 1: Cross Stitch (2 strands)

Anchor		DMC	
1			White
1			White (2 strands)
		032	Pearl Balger Blending Filament (1 strand)
300		745	Yellow–lt.pale
886		677	Old Gold–vy. lt.
4146		754	Peach–lt.
882		407	Pecan
894		223	Shell Pink–med.
22		816	Garnet
44		814	Garnet–dk.
128		800	Delft–pale
921		931	Antique Blue–med.
922		930	Antique Blue–dk.
851		924	Slate Green–vy. dk.
842		3013	Khaki Green–lt.
861		3363	Pine Green–med.
216		367	Pistachio Green–dk.
246		319	Pistachio Green–vy. dk.
879		890	Pistachio Green–ultra dk.
388		3033	Mocha Brown–vy. lt.
899		3782	Mocha Brown–lt.
903		3032	Mocha Brown–med.
273		3787	Brown Gray–dk.
403		310	Black

Step 2: Backstitch (1 strand)

Anchor		DMC	
44		814	Garnet–dk.
922		930	Antique Blue–dk.
273		3787	Brown Gray–dk.
403		310	Black

Step 3: Long Stitch (1 strand)

Anchor		DMC	
22		816	Garnet

Step 4: Beads

		00146	Light Blue

Additional Verse Top

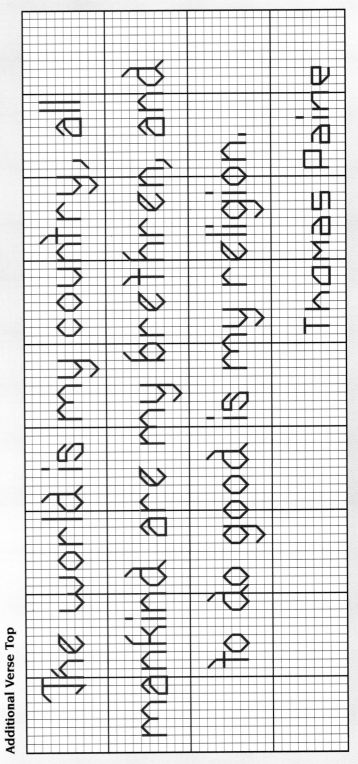

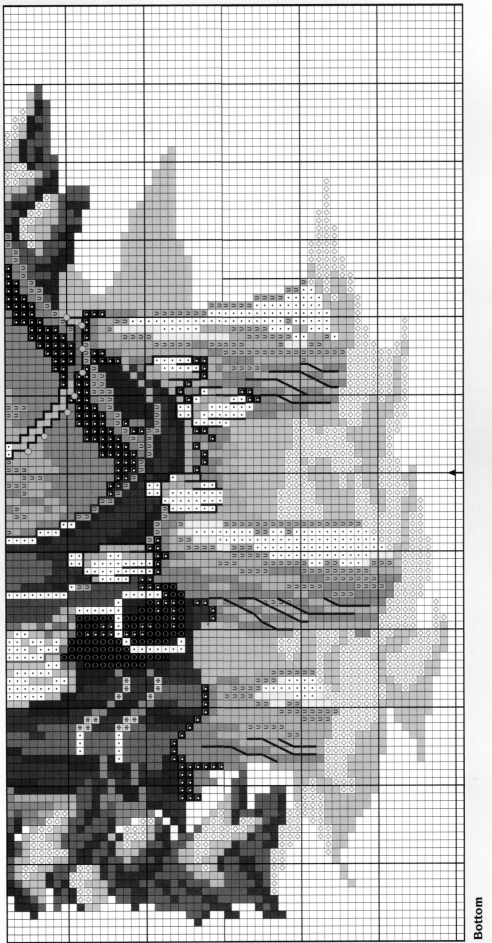

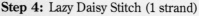

"It is good to be children sometimes and never better than at Christmas."

—Charles Dickens

Photograph on page 96.

Sample Information

The sample was stitched on antique Lavender linen 28 over two threads. The finished design size is 7⅛" x 11⅛". The fabric was cut 14" x 18".

Stitch Count: 116 x 140

Other Fabrics	Finished Size
Aida 11	10" x 14⅛"
Aida 18	6⅛" x 8⅝"
Hardanger 22	5" x 7"

Anchor   DMC

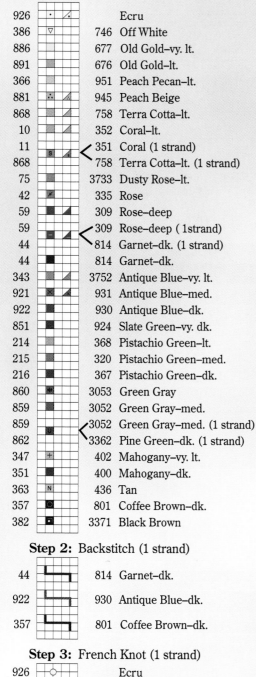

Step 1: Cross Stitch (2 strands)

926		Ecru
386	746	Off White
886	677	Old Gold–vy. lt.
891	676	Old Gold–lt.
366	951	Peach Pecan–lt.
881	945	Peach Beige
868	758	Terra Cotta–lt.
10	352	Coral–lt.
11	351	Coral (1 strand)
868	758	Terra Cotta–lt. (1 strand)
75	3733	Dusty Rose–lt.
42	335	Rose
59	309	Rose–deep
59	309	Rose–deep (1strand)
44	814	Garnet–dk. (1 strand)
44	814	Garnet–dk.
343	3752	Antique Blue–vy. lt.
921	931	Antique Blue–med.
922	930	Antique Blue–dk.
851	924	Slate Green–vy. dk.
214	368	Pistachio Green–lt.
215	320	Pistachio Green–med.
216	367	Pistachio Green–dk.
860	3053	Green Gray
859	3052	Green Gray–med.
859	3052	Green Gray–med. (1 strand)
862	3362	Pine Green–dk. (1 strand)
347	402	Mahogany–vy. lt.
351	400	Mahogany–dk.
363	436	Tan
357	801	Coffee Brown–dk.
382	3371	Black Brown

Step 2: Backstitch (1 strand)

44	814	Garnet–dk.
922	930	Antique Blue–dk.
357	801	Coffee Brown–dk.

Step 3: French Knot (1 strand)

926		Ecru
44	814	Garnet–dk.
343	3752	Antique Blue–vy. lt.

Step 4: Lazy Daisy Stitch (1 strand)

| 216 | 367 | Pistachio Green–dk. |

Additional Verse

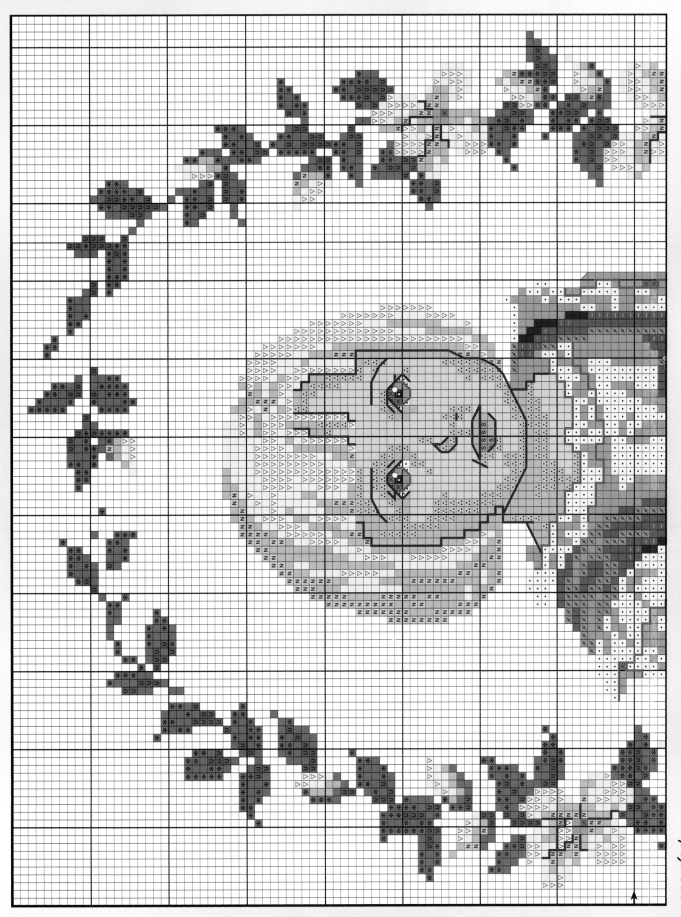

"Blessed are
the peacemakers."
Nathaniel Parker Willis

Saint Francis

...all creatures great and small...the Lord God made them all.

Photograph on page 97.

Sample Information

The sample was stitched on celery Linda 27 over two threads. The finished design size is 8" x 12½". The fabric was cut 14" x 19". Graph begins on page 124.

Stitch Count: 108 x 168

Other Fabrics	Finished Size
Aida 11	9⅞" x 15¼"
Aida 14	7¾" x 12"
Aida 18	6" x 9⅜"
Hardanger 22	4⅞" x 7⅞"

Anchor   DMC

Step 1: Cross Stitch (2 strands)

Anchor	DMC	
1		White
386	3823	Yellow–ultra pale
300	745	Yellow–lt. pale
366	951	Peach Pecan–lt.
881	945	Peach Beige
10	3712	Salmon–med.
11	3328	Salmon–dk. (1 strand)
13	347	Salmon–vy. dk. (1 strand)
892	225	Shell Pink–vy. lt.
893	224	Shell Pink–lt.
13	347	Salmon–vy. dk. (1 strand)
897	221	Shell Pink–vy. dk. (1 strand)
105	209	Lavender–dk.
110	208	Lavender–vy. dk. (1 strand)
101	327	Antique Violet–vy. dk. (1 strand)
110	208	Lavender–vy. dk. (1 strand)
888	3828	Hazel Nut Brown (1 strand)
117	341	Blue Violet–lt.
975	3753	Antique Blue–ultra vy. lt.
159	827	Blue–vy. lt.
160	813	Blue–lt.
859	523	Fern Green–lt.
843	3364	Pine Green
861	3363	Pine Green–med.
842	3013	Khaki Green–lt.
844	3012	Khaki Green–med.
846	3051	Green Gray–dk.
879	500	Blue Green–vy. dk. (1 strand)
861	3363	Pine Green–med. (1 strand)
879	500	Blue Green–vy. dk. (1 strand)
862	934	Black Avocado Green (1 strand)
942	738	Tan–vy. lt.
888	3828	Hazel Nut Brown
309	435	Brown–vy. lt.
310	780	Topaz–vy. dk.
371	433	Brown–med.
381	838	Beige Brown–vy. dk.
382	3371	Black Brown
101	327	Antique Violet–vy. dk. (1 strand)
381	838	Beige Brown–vy. dk. (1 strand)
830	644	Beige Gray–med.
392	642	Beige Gray–dk.
900	648	Beaver Gray–lt.
8581	647	Beaver Gray–med.

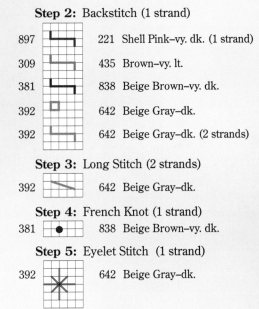

Step 2: Backstitch (1 strand)

Anchor	DMC	
897	221	Shell Pink–vy. dk. (1 strand)
309	435	Brown–vy. lt.
381	838	Beige Brown–vy. dk.
392	642	Beige Gray–dk.
392	642	Beige Gray–dk. (2 strands)

Step 3: Long Stitch (2 strands)

Anchor	DMC	
392	642	Beige Gray–dk.

Step 4: French Knot (1 strand)

Anchor	DMC	
381	838	Beige Brown–vy. dk.

Step 5: Eyelet Stitch (1 strand)

Anchor	DMC	
392	642	Beige Gray–dk.

Additional Verse

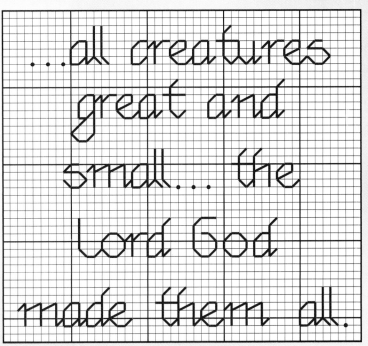

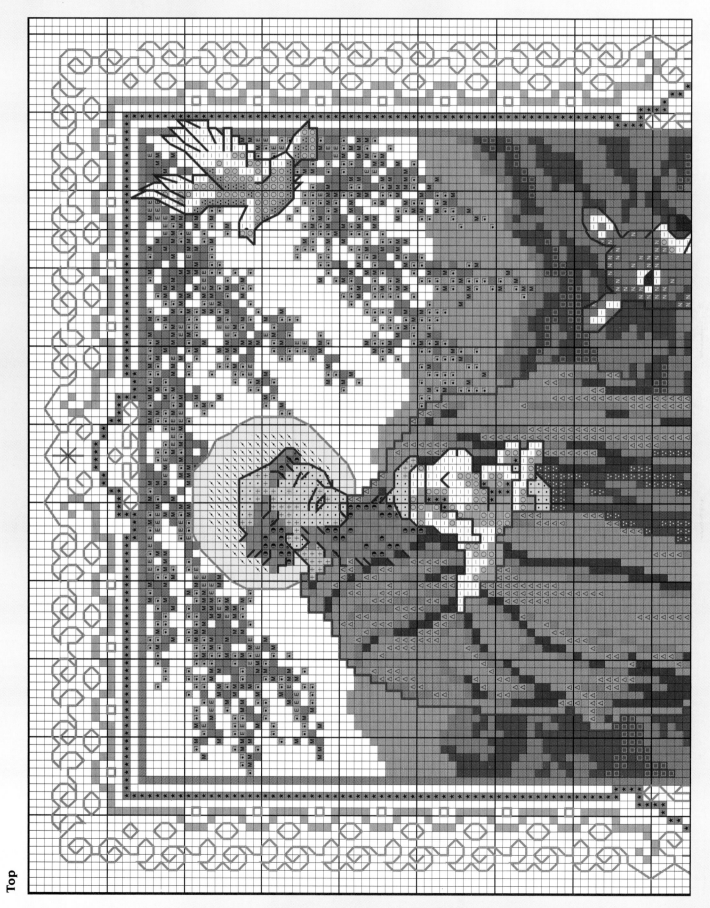

(continued from page 6)

To begin stitching, come up through a hole between woven threads at A. Then, go down diagonally at B. Come back up at C and down at D, etc. Complete the top stitches to create an "X". All top stitches should lie in same direction. Come up at E and go down at B, come up at C and go down at F, etc.

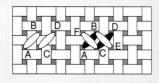

Backstitch

Pull needle through at point marked A. Go down one opening to the right, at B. Then, come back up at C. Now, go down one opening to the right, this time at "A". Continue.

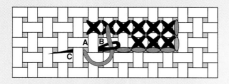

Diamond Eyelet Stitch

This stitch consists of 16 radiating lines. Bring needle up at at 1 and go down at 2 (center). Continue around center 16 times, bringing needle down through center each time.

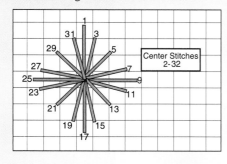

Eyelet Stitch

This stitch consists of eight radiating lines. Bring needle up at at 1 and go down at 2 (center). Continue around center eight times, bringing needle down through center each time.

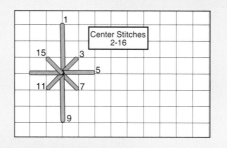

French Knot

Bring needle up at A. Loosely wrap floss once around needle. Place needle at B, next to A. Pull floss taut while pushing needle down through fabric. Carry floss across back of work between knots.

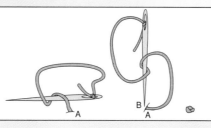

Lazy Daisy

Bring needle up at A. Put needle down through fabric at B and up through at C, keeping floss under needle to form a loop. Pull floss through, leaving loop loose and full. To hold loop in place, go down on other side of thread near C, forming a straight stitch over loop.

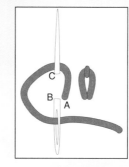

Long Stitch

Bring needle up at A; go down at B. Pull flat. Repeat A–B for each stitch. Length of the stitch should be the same as line length on design chart. This stitch can be horizontal, vertical, or diagonal.

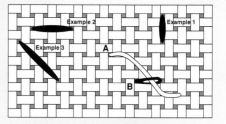

Wrapped Backstitch

Complete Backstitches first. To wrap stitches, come up through fabric just under first stitch. Wrap over first stitch at A and go under second stitch. Be careful not to pierce the fabric or catch the Backstitch. Come up on the opposite side of the stitch at B. Continue wrapping over and under in the same manner. The effect can be varied by how loosely or tightly the floss is pulled when wrapping.

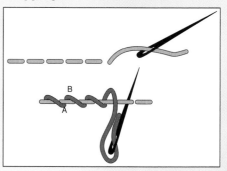

Miracles happen to those who believe in them.

mm-millimetres cm-centimetres
inches to millimetres and centimetres

inches	mm	cm	inches	cm	inches	cm
⅛	3	0.3	9	22.9	30	76.2
¼	6	0.6	10	25.4	31	78.7
½	13	1.3	12	30.5	33	83.8
⅝	16	1.6	13	33.0	34	86.4
¾	19	1.9	14	35.6	35	88.9
⅞	22	2.2	15	38.1	36	91.4
1	25	2.5	16	40.6	37	94.0
1¼	32	3.2	17	43.2	38	96.5
1½	38	3.8	18	45.7	39	99.1
1¾	44	4.4	19	48.3	40	101.6
2	51	5.1	20	50.8	41	104.1
2½	64	6.4	21	53.3	42	106.7
3	76	7.6	22	55.9	43	109.2
3½	89	8.9	23	58.4	44	111.8
4	102	10.2	24	61.0	45	114.3
4½	114	11.4	25	63.5	46	116.8
5	127	12.7	26	66.0	47	119.4
6	152	15.2	27	68.6	48	121.9
7	178	17.8	28	71.1	49	124.5
8	203	20.3	29	73.7	50	127.0

yards to metres

yards	metres	yards	metres	yards	metres	yards	metres	yards	metres
⅛	0.11	2⅛	1.94	4⅛	3.77	6⅛	5.60	8⅛	7.43
¼	0.23	2¼	2.06	4¼	3.89	6¼	5.72	8¼	7.54
⅜	0.34	2⅜	2.17	4⅜	4.00	6⅜	5.83	8⅜	7.66
½	0.46	2½	2.29	4½	4.11	6½	5.94	8½	7.77
⅝	0.57	2⅝	2.40	4⅝	4.23	6⅝	6.06	8⅝	7.89
¾	0.69	2¾	2.51	4¾	4.34	6¾	6.17	8¾	8.00
⅞	0.80	2⅞	2.63	4⅞	4.46	6⅞	6.29	8⅞	8.12
1	0.91	3	2.74	5	4.57	7	6.40	9	8.23
1⅛	1.03	3⅛	2.86	5⅛	4.69	7⅛	6.52	9⅛	8.34
1¼	1.14	3¼	2.97	5¼	4.80	7¼	6.63	9¼	8.46
1⅜	1.26	3⅜	3.09	5⅜	4.91	7⅜	6.74	9⅜	8.57
1½	1.37	3½	3.20	5½	5.03	7½	6.86	9½	8.69
1⅝	1.49	3⅝	3.31	5⅝	5.14	7⅝	6.97	9⅝	8.80
1¾	1.60	3¾	3.43	5¾	5.26	7¾	7.09	9¾	8.92
1⅞	1.71	3⅞	3.54	5⅞	5.37	7⅞	7.20	9⅞	9.03
2	1.83	4	3.66	6	5.49	8	7.32	10	9.14

Index

All of the friends sat quietly and watched as the sun dazzled them and said goodnight.